To Jeff
You...
Margaret Marus

MY MEADOW

❧

"PenRose Publications...a joy forever"

In the creek by my meadow, from the left to right: knee-baby Nell, Odelle, the author, and baby Vi.

MY MEADOW

Margaret Hicks Morris

PenRose
Publishing Company
P.O. Box 620
Mystic Island, New Jersey 08087

Design by Laura Woods, Northern Star Design
Cover design by Laura Woods
Cover and interior drawings by Willie Barr

ISBN 0-9632687-6-7
First Edition

Manufactured in the United States of America
by Quinn-Woodbine Incorporated

CONTENTS

❧

Part One

Goldsboro, North Carolina

T hirtieth Street Station! Philadelphia, Pennsylvania! Thirtieth Street Station! Next stop!" Every word by the conductor was emphasized. My heart began to pound until I thought I could hear it. I was overwhelmed by nostalgia.

I was on my way home from California. I had spent six weeks visiting my grand- and great-grandchildren, and I was daydreaming when the conductor called out, "Thirtieth Street Station!" My mind traveled back to the age of eight when I was on a train with my oldest sister, Nina, coming up north. The train was enormous. I was very excited. I pressed my face against the glass and watched this new and strange landscape roll by.

"Thirtieth Street Station, next stop!" sang the conductor. The train was slowing down. I was sitting on the edge of my seat, my heart pounding. I tried to eat the rest of my sandwich, but I couldn't swallow. "Thirtieth Street Station! Don't leave your luggage! We are here at Thirtieth Street Station, Philadelphia, Pennsylvania!"

The train stopped with a jerk that brought me to my feet. Oh! Lordy! This must be the place where Nina is going to leave me. Everyone else has left me. Mama and Papa and all of my family have left me; and no one has told me why. I guess it was my fault. I thought they all loved me. For over a year and a half my sister Nina has been like a mother to me, and now she is going to leave me, too. I can't let her out of my sight. I'll hold on to her skirt, and I won't let go.

Nina stood up and took our bags and began to walk down the aisle. Why was my heart pounding so? I was filled with anticipation and excitement. I thought I was going to faint. Nina got off the train first, and when it came my turn, I felt myself lifted up by a pair of outstretched arms. Then I saw the most beautiful sight, a sight that can

3

only be duplicated when I get to Heaven and look up into the face of our Savior, Jesus Christ. I found myself in the arms of my Papa and Mama. I thought the joy I felt would kill me. With my arms around Papa in a bear hug, I kissed him and cried. I embraced my parents and vowed I would never be separated again. My brother, Charles, and my sisters, Lucy, Odell, Nell, and baby Vi all kissed me and we cried. It was the first time I had seen my Papa in over two years, and that is a life-time to a child. Mama had been gone a long time, too. The whole family seemed to disappear at separate times. But I have to go back, back to the beginning.

Dash

I was born in Goldsboro, a small town in North Carolina, the third youngest of nine children. My Christian name is Margaret and my middle name is Lee, but my nickname was Mog. We were a big, happy family. We were not rich, but we were rich in love. Papa worked in the foundry. Every morning I would walk Pa to the edge of the road and watch until he was out of sight; he always turned and waved to me three or four times. I would skip back home in the dust. I loved going barefoot in the summer. I can see the dry dust now as it curled up between my toes in the warm, breezy morning.

Back in the house I asked Mama if I could go down in the meadow by the creek. She told me I could; the older children were busy cleaning and helping Mom but, being one of the youngest, I did-n't have to do anything. I had a secret place in the meadow by the creek, and I would run through the grass and wave my arms about. I was going to meet my secret friend.

I sat at the creek and put my feet in the cool, clear water. "Hey Mr. Pudgie!" I called out to a big lazy crawfish that went by. As I sat there, Mrs. Peter Cottontail came by with her babies. I lay down in the meadow and called my make-believe friend, Princess.

"Princess! Oh, there you are! Did you miss me?"

"Yes!" said Princess. "I was bored at the palace, so I came look-ing for you. Pegeen, I want you to come to the palace tomorrow for supper. Can you come?"

"Mog, Mog!" called Mama.

"Bye, Princess. I'll see you tomorrow. I'm coming, Ma!" and I ran as fast as I could back to the house.

"Mog," said Mama, "Take Nell and Baby Vi out under the

pecan tree where I can hear you and play with them while I cook."

"All right, Ma," I said.

I made a place for Nell and Baby Vi to play under the pecan tree. The morning was beautiful, and I could smell the honeysuckle. Our magnolia tree was in bloom, and its aroma was heavenly. We had two bushes that had small red flowers, two pecan trees, and three chinaball trees in the yard. There was a smaller tree where Papa used to pull the small branches for our tooth brushes. Mama always had plenty of flowers and shrubbery. She had plenty of Moses' burning bushes, too. My brother, Charles, would light them to see if they would burn. Many a day when Papa came home he would use the leather strap on Charles. Charles found out those bushes were not divinely blessed like the one Moses encountered.

The leather strap was one hundred and fifty years old and had been passed down from my greatgrandpa to his children. It had been used on Papa's Papa, and in turn he had used it on his thirteen children whenever the occasion called for it. Two generations had felt its sting, and it received the utmost respect. We also had two hickory trees in our yard from which we cut our whipping switch. We learned to respect our parents, and to obey them. My father loved us dearly, but would not hesitate to discipline us.

One time when we all were to line up and get a whipping, Papa took me upstairs and told me he would whip me later. Well, this was in July, and it was very hot. It was early in the morning. I put on a pair of bloomers, every sweater and dress I could find and suffered all day waiting for him to whip me. I nearly died from the heat. Papa forgot to whip me, but I was punished anyway by keeping all those clothes on all day, hiding underneath the porch.

As we sat under the pecan tree I began to tell Nell and baby Vi stories. They enjoyed the stories, but soon grew restless; they wanted June bugs. I went over to the honeysuckle bushes that were loaded with June bugs. I got three June bugs and tied strings on their legs and watched them fly around. In a little while the three of us fell fast asleep. I was awakened by the staccato sound of the July bug as he clattered away in the trees, proclaiming the heat of the day.

"Mog Lee! Mog Lee!" Mama called. "Bring the youngins into eat."

"All right Ma," I answered. Nell and baby Vi were reluctant to wake up, but I persisted and we went into the cool of the house. It was my job to wash their hands. "Ouch!" cried Nell. "Mog's hurt my hands!"

"I have to scrub them good; you were playing with the June bugs. Now come and sit down to lunch and stop bothering Mama."

Mama served my favorite food, black-eyed peas, hot biscuits, and buttermilk.

After lunch, I got out my little book. It was a primer that had been given to me, and I cherished it. It was called *Baby Ray*. I was just in kindergarten and couldn't read yet, but my older sister, Lucy, often read it to me. I was able to memorize the whole book verbatim. Many a friend and relative marveled at my ability to read an entire book at my age. We played on the floor and I would hug my book and tell Nell and Baby Vi about *Baby Ray*.

Soon Charles and my sister came home. They worked at Mr. Ed Kellog's, the white farmer, picking June peas. School was out for the summer, and the children could make a little money by picking and shelling peas. I couldn't wait until I was old enough to go work for Mr. Kellog.

When Papa came home, the children ran to greet him. He usually brought me a flower. Sometimes he brought an injured bird or animal so that I could nurse it back to health. Papa gave Mama his special smile. He patted her face and she blushed. She was embarrassed when he showed her affection in front of the children.

We said a prayer before supper. Mama had cooked turnip greens with side meat (cured), rice, fried ham, red-eye gravy, and corn bread. She cooked on a wood stove, and it gave a special flavor to the food.

Afterward the older girls cleaned up. Papa invited all of us out to the porch to take in the evening. In a short while, Mr. Rue came down the road. He had a white dog with him, and he called Papa to the gate. They spoke for awhile, then Papa opened the gate and the dog came in. Mr. Rue went on down the road.

Papa turned around and, with a big smile said, "Babies, here is your dog!" We all squealed and hollered and nearly scared the poor dog to death. We patted and hugged him.

The dog was young and very friendly. He went to each of us as we called to him, wagging his tail and jumping into our laps. We were used to animals, and knew this little fellow was special

"What shall we call him?" Mama asked. We hollered out names, and finally my brother Charles said, "Why not call him Dash? Look how he dashes about the yard." So, that's how we got Dash. Later that dog literally saved my life.

Sundays

On Saturdays, Papa would start a fire outside under the black iron pot and fill the pot with water. After all the children were scrubbed, the older girls bathed. Baby Vi, Nell, and myself were put to bed while the preparations continued. We slept on a feather mattress and pillows and white sheets Mama had made. The rest of the family cooked for Sunday. Mama often made chicken and dumplings, smothered beef and gravy, rice, collard greens, corn sticks and biscuits, baked sweet potato pie, and peach or apple cobbler. The food was then packed in boxes to be taken to church.

Our Sunday breakfast consisted of fresh milk, hot biscuits, homemade butter-fried apple grits, fried ham or side meat, and fried chicken. Afterward, my older sisters combed out our hair, braided it, and tied on ribbons. Then they helped us into our Sunday dresses; our favorites were made of pongee with wide sashes tied into bows at the back. Our white stockings and black patent leather shoes went on last. We would take a piece of biscuit and rub it on our shoes to shine them. Then we sat in the parlor and waited for Mama and Papa. They were a handsome couple. Mama was a petite, light-skinned woman with long, auburn hair and hazel eyes. Her grandfather had been a white man. Papa was six feet, two inches, dark skinned, as dashing as his eleven brothers. As Mama came into the parlor, we liked to hear the swishing of her starched slip.

Papa was born in Goldsboro, North Carolina, and Mama's family had moved from Rocky Mount, North Carolina. She had one sister, Louise. Mama was only fourteen and Papa was eighteen when they were married. Papa and his brothers had built a little house for the newlyweds. Mama told us years later, when we were grown, that the first three nights of their marriage, Grandma Thornton would take her confused child back home and return with her in the morning. Mama laughed with us when she told this story, but pointed out the tenderness that Papa always showed her—something we would readily expect from this devoutly religious and sensitive man.

Soon Uncle Yag, Papa's brother, came up the road with his horse hitched to a wagon. Papa lifted the little ones onto blankets. The rest of the family drove to church in Papa's big Franklin car. Uncle Yag would stop along the way and pick up several of our cousins, and Papa would pick up one or two relatives.

Soon, in a big clearing, the church appeared, and everyone

grew reverent in its presence. The preacher was standing in the doorway. I was so afraid of him! When he preached, he banged his hands down on the table so hard I thought I would die of fright. He wore all black and was tall as Papa. His sermons were on Moses in the bulrushes, Sidrach, Misach, and Abdenego (the three Hebrew boys in the fiery furnace), or Daniel in the lion's den. He also preached hellfire and damnation, and was always talking about God punishing you. He said that when there was thunder and lightning, God was angry with you. He convinced us that when lightning struck someone, they had been bad and God was angry with them. I was scared of God and almost hated Him because I thought He was mean. I hadn't yet learned about the God of compassion.

At the front of the church there was a big wood stove and rows and rows of hard benches. The children sat on the benches. My legs could hardly touch the floor. Church services lasted all day. Sometimes a child would fall asleep and roll off the hard benches onto the floor. When we got older, we didn't dare go to sleep or we would get a spanking. The church was soon full, and it seemed everyone around me was a cousin. Papa, Uncle Bubba, and all the other uncles were sitting up front, singing. They all were deacons and could those brothers sing.

Mama held baby Vi in her lap, and knee-baby Nell sat sucking her finger between Mama and me. Nell was two years younger than me, and baby Vi was four years younger. I looked up adoringly at Mama. Her hair was pinned up in a bun, and her pongee dress was very pretty.

Papa and his brothers had wonderful singing voices. Papa and the congregation used tambourines and clapped their hands. I could hear Papa's tenor voice rise above everyone else. Then my sister Odell began to play the piano and sing. She taught herself. She had a beautiful soprano voice. As the song "Nearer My God to Thee" rang out, the "Amens" and "Yes, Lords" could be heard throughout the church. I could see the preacher getting stirred up, and I knew he was going to talk about that fiery place underground where that ugly man in a red suit with a pitchfork was going to get me. Then he would talk about God in Heaven. The preacher opened his Bible at random and started to talk. It wasn't until much later that I realized the Preacher could not read or write.

There were a lot of people in the congregation that could not read or write. It took me a long time to realize my Mama and Papa could not read or write, but they all understood they had to live good and Godly lives. They could count money, and no one could cheat them. After I was able to read and write, I took it upon myself to read to Mama and Papa. I read the Bible slowly to them, and I made it a habit to read the Bible from beginning to the end.

The preacher stood up and began, "My dear chillins. It is such a beautiful day that God has given us. He's smiling down on us right now." Then the preacher pointed up, and my eyes went right to the ceiling. And there in the corner sitting on a beam was the biggest possum I have ever seen. I was so startled. In my imagination, God had turned into a possum! Didn't the preacher say God was looking down on us.

The preacher cleared his throat and began to preach about the three Hebrew boys. He was really worked up now; he was foaming at the mouth. He heaved up and down, and when those Hebrew boys were thrown into the fiery furnace, I began to cry for them. The preacher said, "They are safe out of that burning hell. They have been rescued by Divine Providence."

The ushers took up a collection and then called for the mourners' bench to be put in place. It was about midafternoon now. You could see parents pushing their teenage children up front, and they began a soulful mourn. It went on and on. Then the preacher got excited again and began to foam at the mouth. One little boy at the altar opened his eyes and screamed, "Mad dog!" and the mourners at the bench scattered.

After the preacher dismissed us, we went outside. Tablecloths were spread on homemade tables. Then a feast was laid out: collard greens, turnip greens, cabbage-fried chicken, stewed chicken, chicken and dumplings, ham, fried side meat, spareribs, stewed beef, chittlins, potato salad, corn pudding, rice pudding, bread pudding, riced Irish potatoes, biscuits, corn bread. Whole cake bread was cooked in a skillet on a fire; watermelons had been put in the creek to keep cold. There would be jelly cake, butter cake, coconut cake. There would be homemade roast beef and lemonade and spiced drink. This happened every Sunday.

After eating, the young teenage boys disappeared down at the creek. They didn't want the preacher to start up the mourner bench again! The women would sit around and talk about their husbands and children. Some of the men would disappear into the woods. I went down by the creek and sat behind a tree. I saw the preacher and one of the men take a brown jug out of the creek and lift it to their shoulders and drink from it. They made ugly faces and the preacher said, "Now this is the real white lightning!"

Mothers began calling their children together. Everyone began to pack their food. The congregation stood in a circle and waited for the preacher so we could sing and Reverend would pray. My Papa said loudly, "Where's Reverend Lipscomb?!" And I called out in the loudest voice, "He's down at the creek with Mr. Rue drinking white lightning out of a brown jug!" Everyone froze, and I realized I had done something wrong. I could see some of the grownups smiling. Mama said rather firmly, "Youngin', hush ya mouth!" Uncle Bubba, who was a deacon, gave the prayer, and by the time Reverend and Mr. Rue got back, we were all loading up.

We fell asleep on the ride home. I remember being lifted into Papa's arms and taken into the house. Mama put us in bed on the soft feather mattress. Baby Vi and knee-baby Nell and I slept together. I could faintly hear Mama come in during the night and pat each of us. She would take each of us to the chamber pot if we needed it. I could feel her in the room, and I remember hearing her say, "Lord, take care of my youngins." I still say the same prayer for my children and grandchildren and greats.

During the Week

I would be awakened by the smell of sour milk biscuits and side meat cooking downstairs. I heard Papa pass our door, and I hurried up and went downstairs so I could eat with Papa and Mama, and Papa always let me dunk my biscuits in his coffee. They always got up about 5:30 AM, and by 6:30 Papa was on his way to work.

Papa worked in a foundry, to which he walked every day. He was a hard worker and respected by the bosses and fellow workers. It was difficult work but provided his large family with most of its needs, since we grew vegetables and raised pigs and chickens for our food. Mama made our clothes and we all pitched in to work at home and to care for the youngins.

I remember in those early days, when I was about seven, that Papa was laid off from his job. It wasn't his fault. The family seemed so close together, and Uncle Yag told Papa to bring the family and help pick his cotton patch. The next day, Mama and Papa packed us in the car, and away we went. Nina went to wrap tobacco at farmer Kellog's.

We arrived at the farm and we kissed everyone. Mama spread the blanket under the big poplar tree. Lucy, Odell, Charles, and Mama and Papa picked cotton. They all stopped for lunch and we had fun. We would put the boll weevils on our hand and they would sting us. The cotton bags were real long. Many a day was spent under that tree while our parents picked cotton. Finally Papa was called back to the foundry.

Our older brother Charles was a great tease. He'd tease my older sisters when my parents were not around. He was the only boy, and he was very spoiled. Before lunch, he came into the kitchen carrying knee-baby Nell and baby Vi and he put them on the floor with me. Lucy, my second oldest sister, came and washed our hands and faces, and she helped Mama to feed us. Everyone sat down and Mama said grace and prayed. Charles made a funny face, and I giggled and everyone looked at me.

Charles and Odell were the cause of my getting punished. They would make the funniest faces at the wrong times. I soon learned how to stay away from them. The oldest ones cleaned the kitchen and then went off to shell June peas at farmer Kellog's.

With nine in the family, Mama always had a big laundry to do. She usually washed on Monday. The older girls helped. Charles made a fire outside under the black pot. Usually we had two big black pots on the fire. Mama never owned a washing machine. She washed our clothes by hand on a washing board.

She would boil the white clothes in one of the pots. She would put bluing in the pot and the clothes were sparkling white. Ma starched everything, even the pillow cases. I always wondered how Mama did it as long as she did.

Thank God her health was good, for she always had so much to do. Mama made us dresses from the sacks the chicken feed came in; they usually had flowers on them. She made all of our slips and underwear out of unbleached muslin and homespun material. She would sew lace on our dresses. She would wash and bleach the material and starch everything. Mom made our sheets and bedspreads and all our curtains. She made our feather mattresses and pillows. We raised all our vegetables and our chickens and pigs. We didn't have to buy much of anything. Mama even made our soap. Our bath soap smelled so good; she would take rose blossoms, magnolia blossoms, and honeysuckle and do something with them and put it in our bath soap.

While playing in the yard, we could hear the sound of a train's whistle off in the distance and the "Choo, choo, choo" of its engine and the clack of its wheels as it passed over the trestle. The trestle passed over my creek. Whenever I heard a train, I would feel so lonely and sad. I looked toward the trestle. I could not see the train, but I knew it was there. I could see the steam and smoke above the trees as it passed. I ran into the house and hugged my Mama real tight around the legs. The sound of a train's whistle would always make me shudder; it is still the same today.

Many a mid-morning, I would look down the road and see my favorite aunt coming down the lane with her two youngins. They were knee-baby Nell's and baby Vi's ages. I called Mama and she and I went to meet Aunt LuAnn Hicks. She and Mama hugged each other. She was Mama's closest friend. She and Mama married two brothers, so Mama and Aunt LuAnn were like sisters. We all came into our house and as the children began to play and Mama and Auntie Lu talked, I asked, "Mama. Could I play in the meadow!" She said, "Yes." I was glad because I hadn't talked to my secret friend for a long time.

As I skipped along, I broke a piece of honeysuckle vine off, and a hummingbird followed me. I saw Mrs. Peter Cottontail and her family. I stopped and spoke to her. I saw Papa Chipmunk with a nut in his mouth. He was taking breakfast to his family. I hurried to the creek and put my feet in the water. Soon the crawfish were all around my feet. I saw a lot of minnows and tadpoles. Mr. Frog was no doubt calling his family. He called, "Ribit, ribit, croak, croak!" "Princess, Princess," I called to my make-believe friend. Soon she appeared. "Oh Pegeen! I missed you! We had a beautiful party at the palace, and I wore a dress made of gold. Everyone told me how pretty I was, and Prince Charming kissed me. Come, I'm going to take you to the palace." Princess and I went to the palace. She put on her gold dress and she gave me one made of all precious jewelry. It was my favorite color, blue. I had on golden slippers, and we played all over the palace. Prince Charming came and danced with me. I heard Mama calling me, so I said goodbye to my make-believe friend, Princess.

I went running across the meadow. I called Dash and he came to meet me. Auntie Lu was getting ready to go home with her children, and we all walked down the road with her, and Mama said, "We will walk farther down and meet Papa." Oh! I was happy as we children walked barefoot in the dust. I heard the family's private whistle and I knew Papa saw us. We three younger ones hadn't learned the private whistle, but Papa said he was going to teach me before school opened. It would be quite an occasion as all of the relatives would gather, and the ones who had not learned the private family whistle would learn it. That whistle was used in emergencies and cases of danger. It was used to send messages. As I grew older, I realized it could be relayed for miles. When the whistle was given, the whole family showed up.

When Papa came by, he hugged Auntie Lu and kissed all of us. We said our goodbyes to Auntie, and we walked back down the road. Papa put knee-baby Nell on his shoulder. Mama carried baby Vi, and Dash and I ran along the dusty road with the warm, sweet breeze caressing my face. When we arrived home, my sisters and brother were home from farmer Kellog's. The girls were setting the table. Mama usually cooked during the day when she cleaned house. I still do the same today, but I have a hard time getting my daughters to do the same. It saves a lot of time. After supper, we all went out on the porch, and Papa cut the biggest watermelon. Mama would bring out her homemade root beer. Some of the family would come by, and Papa and his brothers practiced their group singing (all twelve brothers and one sister). They only had tambourines. It sounded so good. All the neighbors would come and sit in the yard and on the porch all the time they rehearsed. The grownups would sit and drink cherry wine that Papa and his brothers made every year. It was so nice. Even though all these years have passed, I can still hear them singing—I remember those beautiful days. Oh! How I loved those beautiful, lazy, uncomplicated days.

Church Picnic

It was time for our church picnic held at Uncle Yag's big farm. Everyone was cooking for days. My brother and older sisters would walk to the farm. Uncle Yag sent his big horse and wagon to pick up people along the way.

Uncle Yag had a big delicious apple orchard. He had pecan trees and, like his brothers, he raised pigs on his farm. In back of a big poplar tree, there were two whole pigs being barbecued. There were fried chickens, baked yams, potato salad, all kinds of greens, corn bread, homemade root beer, lemonade, stewed tomatoes, corn on the cob, and all kinds of cakes and pies.

After we ate, we played games such as spring board, baseball, horse shoes, and jump rope. Then the men would see which of their dogs would come to the picnic after hearing the family whistle. Each one of my uncles whistled, and soon a cloud of dust rose up on the road. We saw each dog run down the road and they seemed to sense it was a contest. We all squealed when we saw our Dash in the lead. We gave the dogs cool water and food to eat.

Some of my uncles lived at least two miles apart, but all of us recognized that whistle, and to this day it plays a big part in our lives.

We all sang songs and Reverend Lipscomb gave a sermonette about friends enjoying times together. He couldn't preach long because he had been eating the whole time we were there. After picnics and Sunday church, he was loaded up with so much food. That Baptist preacher could eat some fried chicken!

I hated to leave because Uncle Yag and Auntie Lu and their family were my favorites. All the dogs walked beside the wagon; all the teenagers walked beside the wagon or in back of it. We all arrived back home very happy and sleepy. After a beautiful day, Mama and Papa would sit in the kitchen and talk about the day's events. Usually baby Vi or knee-baby Nell would have an accident in bed, and I would go in and tell Mama, and she would come and change everyone into dry clothes.

Aunt Louise Thornton

Mama and the older children began to clean the house. My brother Charles swept the dirt about the house. Mama's plants and flowers stood out beside the broom-clean yard. Mama took our mattresses and pillows out in the yard to air them. She scrubbed the floor in our room and washed the windows. She made new curtains out of some material she called homespun. She told knee-baby Nell and baby Vi and me that her sister Louise from up north was coming for a visit. It had been nearly two years since we had seen her. We were very excited because she always brought us such beautiful gifts. We cleaned and cleaned. Mama opened the parlor and the Sunday eating room. The furniture in the eating room and kitchen had been made by Papa and his brothers. There was a beautiful shine to the wood. Today that furniture would be worth a fortune. Mama cooked and cooked a lot of goodies. She dressed us all up and combed our hair.

The entire family sat on the porch, and finally we saw a cloud of dust down the road. Mama shaded her eyes and stood up. As the cloud came nearer, Mama and Papa went down in the yard. Then a big black car pulled into our yard, and this woman that looked like Mama stepped out. It was my Aunt Louise from New Jersey. She had long, auburn hair that was waved and hazel eyes like Mama. She had on the prettiest silk dress and she carried a white hat. She was very light-skinned, and her smile was brilliant.

After greeting all of us, she introduced her chauffeur, Mr. Sam. He began to take box after box from the car. We were excited and eager to know what was in those boxes. The older children went into the house to set the table in the Sunday eating room. I asked Auntie Louise if she had any books. I have always been interested in reading books. Later on in my teens, I would read a book a day in the summer months. Auntie told me she had some books for me, and she would give them to me after the boxes were opened.

Mama called us in for supper. Auntie went to her room and Mama took our prettiest pitcher and wash basin to her room. Charles brought her warm water so she could wash up for supper. Over in the corner, Mama had gotten out the company chamber pot. We didn't have a bathroom. We had an outhouse that had been scrubbed clean. Oh how Charles hated to clean it! When Mama would occasionally work at the white ladies' homes, she would bring the Sunday paper home. Papa would take the comics and paper the inside walls of the outhouse. I became well acquainted with Little Orphan Annie, Daddy Warbucks, and Annie's dog, Sandy, Andy Gump, and Popeye while sitting on the throne in the outhouse.

After everyone finished eating, Mama brought out dessert and we ate on the porch. Mama had made Auntie Louise's favorite, sweet potato pudding and lemonade. Papa had gone to the ice house and bought some ice, chopped it, and put it in our glasses. Ice was a luxury to us. Our ice boxes were made of wood, so we had to buy ice. Papa wrapped the ice in paper and towels to make it last.

We didn't have electricity at our home in the country. We had several kerosene lamps and candles. I couldn't wait to get old enough to wash the lamp shades. They were the cause of most of my whippings because I broke so many. I was glad when we moved and got electricity.

We had a very beautiful first-day visit with Auntie Louise and Mr. Sam. Oh, could that man eat! They stayed with us for ten long, summer days. I finally found out what was in those boxes. There were gifts for everyone, and always a big amount of money for Mama and

Papa. Fifty dollars at that time was a fortune. Auntie Louise brought Mama two pretty silk dresses and some shoes. She brought Charles and Papa some shirts and socks. All the other girls she gave dresses and stockings, but she gave me two dresses and a little purse, white slippers and socks, a notebook, pencils, and some reading books: *The Adventures of Huckleberry Finn, Brer Rabbit,* the *Holy Bible*, and a book called a dictionary. We all were very sad and tearful when Auntie Louise left.

An Encounter

Little did I know that the next day after Auntie Louise left was going to change my life. My carefree, long, beautiful, happy summer days would be interrupted by something so horrible that it affected my whole life. I still can remember each moment even though it was sixty-eight years ago.

That morning started out as it usually did. I got up early with Mama and Papa, and I dunked my biscuit in Papa's coffee. I helped Mama pack Papa's lunch box, then walked with him to the edge of the road, where he kissed me goodbye. I kicked the dust between my toes as I went down the path home. I could hear the July bugs begin to clatter, clatter clack. I helped Mama a while, then asked her if she wanted me to awaken knee-baby Nell and baby Vi. She said to let them sleep. I asked her if could I go back down to the creek and meadow and she said, "Just for a while."

I went skipping across the meadow through the soft, light brown grass. Mama used to cut some of this grass, beat the fuzz off, and tie it up to use as a broom.

The blue birds and hummingbirds were flying very low overhead. I was excited because I was going to see my make-believe friend, Princess. I hadn't seen her for such a long time because I wanted to stay close to home while Auntie Louise was there. Butterflies danced and flitted all around me. One settled on my arm and hitchhiked all the way to the creek. When I got to the creek, I saw a pony tethered to a tree. So often people would tether their horses in the creek if they had sores or cuts on their legs. Often I would splash water on their legs. I loved horses. I went in the creek and patted the horse for a while, then I sat on the bank and put my feet in the water. I laid back on the soft grass as the minnows tickled my toes. I closed my eyes and called my little imaginary friend, "Princess!"

She came and said, "Pegeen. Where have you been? I've looked for you so long."

"What are we going to do today?" I asked.

Just then, a large airplane went by overhead. "Oh! Let's go on a plane ride" she said.

"All right! Let's go Princess!" In my mind, we called the plane back and rode around the white cottony clouds.

Then the light shifted and I felt a dark shadow pass across me. I looked up, and my heart nearly stopped, for standing at my head was the largest white man I had ever seen. He had a horrible look on his face. I hadn't been in contact with many white people. I stood up very slowly. I was terrified. I turned to run but he caught me by the arm. I couldn't move. He was hurting my arm. I began to whimper. He pushed me to the ground. "Oh God!" I thought. "He's going to kill me!" He grabbed my dress by the top and began to tear it off my body. I began to cry louder and he told me to hush or he would kill me. I was about to die from fright. I screamed, "Dash! Dash! Dash!" As he raised his fist to hit me, he was knocked over by a tremendous force. It was Dash. Dash was tearing him to pieces. I screamed and screamed. I heard Mama and Charles running, calling my name. The white man scrambled to his feet and ran. Dash chased him for a while, then turned back. By the time Charles and Mama found me, I was half naked and incoherent.

Charles ran to look for the man, but he couldn't find him. Charles stooped to pick me up, and I cringed away from him. Mama hugged me and cried, and I finally allowed Charles to pick me up. He brought me in the house, then went off to the factory to get Papa. Not only did Papa come home, but all of his brothers that worked there came as well. After they came and saw me, they all cried. Some of the brothers went outside, and each took turns blowing our family whistle to the north, south, east, and west. In less than a half hour, over fifty relatives gathered at the house. They brought long barrel guns, axes, and a lot of dogs. They searched the meadow and creek from end to end. It is very good that they didn't find him. But the man had his problems too. An inmate of a mental hospital in our town, he had wandered away. He lived out the rest of his life in the institution.

In the meantime, Mama and the ladies washed me up. I was still in shock and quite incoherent. They began to ask me questions; "What did he do to me?" I couldn't answer. Mama took me in her arms and held me.

Papa wouldn't let everyone come in to see me, because I was beginning to be embarrassed. I couldn't understand why anyone wanted to hurt me. I had always been kind and thoughtful. It was years before I realize what that man was trying to do. I thank God for our dog Dash. He served us well and faithfully until he died of old age.

Family Whistle

The morning after my encounter in the meadow, Papa called me and asked me if I was going to eat with him and walk him down the road. I said, "No, Papa." He came into the bedroom and patted my face and kissed me and said, "Don't you worry baby. No one will ever hurt you again as long as I live." I wouldn't let Papa touch me for a few days.

I was afraid to go on the porch and in the yard. I stayed in the house as much as possible. I played in the house with knee-baby Nell and baby Vi. For days I wouldn't turn Mama's skirts loose.

About two weeks after that horrible incident, I went to the kitchen window. Looking out on the yard, I saw Mama Cottontail with her bunnies. The rabbit had blood on her leg. I ran outside and picked up the rabbit and saw that her leg was broken. I put a bandage on it and built a pen for her and her bunnies and gave them some food. I told Dash not to let anyone bother them; the dog and rabbit got along well.

I stayed out in the yard a long time. I felt safe as long as Dash was there with me. We all ate lunch and waited for Papa to come home. I ventured up the path with Dash. Papa came and kissed me and took my hand and we went home. The girls fixed supper because Mama was teaching them how to be good housewives.

After supper, Papa and Mama called us onto the porch. Papa said it was time for knee-baby Nell and me to learn the family's private whistle. I had been trying it by myself and was able to pick it up rather easily. When it came time for knee-baby Nell to do it, all she could do was spit. We laughed so hard that she began to cry. Mama told her she could wait for two or three more years.

Papa called Charles and me out to the yard. He began to teach me how to defend myself. The older girls could fight like tigers; they could throw Papa and Charles over their shoulders. They were terrific. Charles really had it tough because he had to train six sisters in the art of self-defense. When Papa and Charles finished, we could stand up to the best of them—man or woman. Charles taught us how to kick and box.

All my relatives knew how to defend themselves. There was a saying where we lived, "Don't bother that clan!" It was a dangerous world, and it was important to know how to survive in it. I was a passive person and didn't like hurting anyone, but I was glad I had the skills to protect myself if the situation called for it.

The Octagon Man

We all were very excited the next day because the Octagon man was coming around. Twice a year he would come around with books, notebooks, pencils, erasers, rulers, everything for school. Parents would save coupons from Octagon soap products and exchange them for various articles. Sometimes we were allowed to ask neighbors who did not have children for their coupons. Sometimes my brother and sisters would do errands and small jobs for them. When the Octagan Man came, we still had one more month before school. Mom had saved enough coupons so I could get a tablet and two pencils. I was so proud of my things. The Octagon man would stay in front of our house a half a day, and we children would show off our things.

School

It was almost time for us to go to school. I was entering the first grade. I had learned to read rather well by now, and I was looking forward to classes.

The first day of school arrived. I was so proud to be going to school. I wore the new shoes and outfit Aunt Louise had given me. I had my new notebook and pencil. Charles and Nina would not be going to school this year; they had jobs and Papa said they could keep working, so the other children, except knee-baby Nell and baby Vi, went to school. The day was delightful. My teacher, Mrs. Phillips, was a very nice person, and she was pleased that I could read and write. My older sisters taught me. From that day on, all my life I had a strong love for learning.

The long, beautiful summer went into fall, and finally fall turned into winter. When I came home from school I liked telling Mama what I had learned. Then I would change my clothes and play with Dash in the yard. I was still frightened to go to the meadow and creek. In the yard I looked at the rabbit and her bunnies. Her leg had healed, so I took her to the edge of the meadow and turned her and her family loose. Dash and I went back home, and I tried calling my imaginary friend, Princess, but she never came to me after that incident in the meadow. Princess and I always had a lot of love for each other. Our friendship, even though it was imaginary, was of love, so when such violence entered our beloved meadow, it shattered our bond of love, and drove her away for good. I went in the yard and pulled up some grass and shook the dirt out of the long root and washed the root. It looked like long blond hair. I would tie the hair back and put a cloth on the grass part and make a doll. Sometimes I would make whole families of them. I was very lonely. I missed Princess so much. I would go a short distance into the meadow. I would always take Dash with me. In our yard there was a tall sycamore tree. I used to climb to the top limb with my book and sit up there for hours reading and daydreaming. Dash would sit under the tree. I loved climbing trees, and I would pick the tallest trees to climb. I would look over my meadow and creek and feel sad about my dear friend Princess.

Wonderful Autumn

The beautiful days were rolling by. We would go to church on Sundays. We did not have picnics in the fall and winter. We would have a long service. The singing by Papa and his brothers was beautiful. We would go home in Papa's car and have a special Sunday dinner. Papa and Mama were a team of good providers. Papa and Mama liked to fish, and it was fun to see them bring fresh fish home and cook them. Before winter came he would harvest the greens, sweet potatoes, and other food he and Mama had grown. He would dig a ten-foot by six-foot pit in the back yard and line it with leaves and branches, and straw and hay. He would put all of the excess foods from the big garden in the pit, and he would make a top for it and line it in the same material that he lined the sides. This way he could store food to be used throughout the winter. That is where Mama would store her homemade root beer, too. Papa would put baskets of delicious apples from Uncle Yag's orchard in the pit.

Nina was old enough to have a boyfriend. After dinner they would sit in the parlor. Nina was very pretty. She was tall and thin and had hair down to her waist. In her blue dress with pleats all around the bottom, she was a knockout. We all went out and sat on the porch. Soon Nina and her friend would walk down the road and back. Finally, Papa told him it was time to go home; he went. Charles teased Nina so bad she gave him an uppercut, and he left her alone.

Everyone then changed their clothes, and Charles got the hard ball and two gloves. He and Papa would have a catch, and then we would take turns catching and throwing the ball. Many a time our cousins would play against us. We became so good at baseball playing that people began coming to see us play. Little did we know, we sisters would later be asked for autographs because of our fame for playing baseball.

The Holidays

Soon there was a feeling of excitement in the air as Thanksgiving and Christmas drew near. Mama began to bake her jelly cakes and pineapple cakes, butter cakes and coconut cakes. On Thanksgiving Papa would go to Uncle Yag's farm and kill one of our geese. Mama would stuff and bake it, and we would sit in the Sunday eating room. Before supper Papa prayed and asked the blessing. All of us had to thank God for something. Sometimes on holidays, company came by. Odell would play the piano and we would all sing. We all went back to school quite happy because we knew Christmas would soon be here.

We began to practice for our Christmas play at our church. Odell, knee-baby Nell, and I sang "Silent Night." Odell had the most beautiful voice. I made the angel costumes for that Christmas.

Papa would go to the store and buy a whole stalk of bananas. There would be about a hundred bananas on one stalk. We hung it on the back porch so our company could pull one whenever they wanted. Mama did all of that wonderful cooking, and of course the house was impeccably clean.

Papa had cut a tree, and we hung our stockings over the fireplace in the parlor. We had been told if we were bad Santa Claus would bring switches. They didn't have to worry about me, because I had a healthy respect for the strap and switches!

It was hard for us to go to sleep on Christmas Eve. Knee-baby Nell, baby Vi, and I were sent to bed early; the older ones were able to stay up late with Mama and Papa.

Mama called us the next morning. We tried to eat breakfast,

but we couldn't, so finally Mama told us to go in the parlor and see what Santa had brought us. We squealed as we ran to our pile of goodies. I looked in my stocking; there were two oranges, apples, cracker jacks, and candy. Over on my chair there was a new dress, patent leather shoes, one pair of sneakers, mittens and scarf, pencils and reading books, and hair ribbons. We didn't get many toys, but we were very happy with the things we received. Mama made me an apron; it was just like hers. I was a little hurt because knee-baby Nell and baby Vi received doll babies and I didn't.

After a while, Papa called us outside. It was a very mild day. We didn't have severe cold winters at that time. We had snow once in a while, but it didn't last long because of the mild climate. Once outside, we saw Dash playing with a pretty white horse. Papa said, "Here is a present for everyone!" I patted the horse and Papa put a blanket on her. He put knee-baby Nell, baby Vi, and me on the horse and walked us down the road with Dash running beside us. It was so much fun, I didn't want to get off.

Knee-baby Nell asked, "What is her name?" and Papa said we had to name her. Lucy said, "Call him Nag!" We said, "No!" Charles said, "Let's call her Maude because we know Mog will have her all the time and we can say Mog and Maude!" Odell laughed. I said, "Yes! Yes!" and that is how we named our horse Maude.

We enjoyed that Christmas day very much. In the late afternoon, Papa loaded us on Maude, and he and Mama and the big children walked over to Uncle Yag's farm. Uncle Bubba and his family came over also, and we had a good time eating homemade ice cream and cake. Uncle Yag gave us more apples and a large bag of cracklins. Papa, Uncle Yag, and Uncle Bubba made plans for hog killing on New Year's Day.

All of the brothers raised pigs on Uncle Yag's farm. Every Saturday for a month, at least three of the brothers would kill a pig, and the brothers and their wives would make sausage, liver pudding, and dress the pigs for curing. The chitterlins would be cleaned; some would be used for sausage casings and some for cooking. There would be three big, black, cast-iron pots on the wood fire outside cooking fat for making lard and cracklins. There would be greens cooked, black-eyed peas, rice, and baked yams. The black-eyed peas would be cooked with a cured hog's head. There was always sour milk biscuits and corn bread. On New Year's Day, a man had to go to your home first, or that home would have bad luck. Papa and Mama would bring their meat home, and Papa would salt and brine it down, season it, and put it in our curing shed. Oh! The heavenly smell when that meat was cooked after it was cured!

The Move

Papa came home from work one day quite upset. He called Mama off to the side, and, when she finished cooking, she told us we had to move. Our landlord, Mr. Jampson, wanted his home. He gave us a month to move. We were very sad because we loved where we lived. Papa said we would have to find another large home with a lot of land so we could keep Maude, our horse.

A few days later, we packed our car and drove to another part of Goldsboro nearer to town. We saw this big white house with a lot of land out back and a swing on the porch. The front yard was small because the house was about twenty feet from the unpaved road. There were homes right across the road from us. This home would have to be cleaned all the time because of the dust.

The people across the street did not have children. They had a huge apple tree in their yard, and some of the branches extended halfway over the road. Some of our new neighbors said the lady who owned the tree, Miss Laura, was mean and didn't want anyone to keep the apples that fell in the street. The children in the neighborhood would pick them up out of the road anyhow, and she would come out and yell at them. Mama told us never to pick the apples in the street, but if any apples happened to fall into our yard from the branches that extended, then we could keep them. Many a day I would sit under one of those branches and say, "Fall apple— fall!"

Miss Laura was always peeping from behind her curtain. She came across the street one day and said we couldn't keep Maude in our back yard. Mama called her in the house and introduced the family, and when she saw me she said, "This is the little 'fall apple fall' girl!" Everyone had a big laugh out of that. Mama offered Miss Laura some coffee and cake. She firmly refused to accept any food from anyone.

She took a liking to my older sister Nina. She told her how pretty she was. She told all the girls except me how pretty they were. You can imagine how bad I felt. My feelings were hurt. Everybody in town disliked Miss Laura. I tried to make friends with her, but she told me not to touch her fence. She thought she knew everything that went on in the neighborhood because she kept a watchful eye from behind her curtain. Her husband, Mr. Anthony, was very nice and he and my Papa went fishing. Our family was fond of Mr. Anthony.

Little did we know that many years later, after Mama and Mr. Anthony had passed away, that Miss Laura would marry Papa. She came to Mama's funeral, and a few months later she married my Papa. The sisters wore the same black mourning outfits that we had worn to Mama's funeral to Papa and Miss Laura's wedding. I heard many a person say Papa could not help himself. They said Miss Laura always had some power to get people to do what she wanted.

The Klan

Slowly, we settled comfortably into our new neighborhood. Then one night while we were outside, we heard screaming up the road. We saw several men in white sheets walking, going into homes. They were the Klu Klux Klan, and Papa and Mama took us inside and closed the doors.

Papa closed our bedroom door. He put his gun inside the door. I peeped through the crack, and I saw Charles with a long-barreled gun. Mama was praying. I thought my heart would stop. All my older sisters had big sticks of wood Papa had carved for baseball bats. Only through the Lord's mercy were we not consumed that night.

We didn't have locks on our doors then. The KKK came on our porch and pushed the door open. Papa stood in front of them, all six feet two of him, and Charles behind him. Papa said, "What can I do for you?" They started to push past Papa, but Papa looked as if he grew taller, and he didn't give an inch. One of them said, "We are looking for that damn nigger Tom Cherry!"

"As we just recently moved here," Papa said, "we don't know him or any of the neighbors. If you want to search, go ahead. I can't stop all of you, but don't frighten my family!" They looked so bewildered they backed off the porch and moved onto another house.

Mama had her Bible in her hand, and it was opened, and Charles went to Mama's side and said, "Mama, you have turned to the 23rd Psalm," and Mama said, "That's the prayer I was saying!"

You remember now, Mama couldn't read, but after I grew up and remembered that incident, I can see there was a supernatural air about the whole thing.

24

The next day, I sneaked over to farmer Kellog's and looked for Charles. I didn't see him, so I walked around the barn looking at all the farm equipment. I leaned on a post and dislodged a large board in the hay loft. It fell down, and there was a ten-inch, splinter sticking out. It hit my leg and stuck in. We were not allowed in the hospital. We could only use the back door at the doctor's. He had to cut the wood out of my leg. I carry that ten-inch scar today in my left leg.

A few days later, there was a lynching down in a place that was called Lynch Hollow; there were great big trees growing down there, but there was one particular tree that was used for lynching. I saw it once, and after hearing so many bad things about it, I began to hate it. I actually saw a devil in that tree.

One day a rumor spread around town that the tree had been cut down. Sometime later at a family gathering, I heard Papa and his brothers say they were going to cut the other two trees down. Those men were not afraid of anything. I didn't like my new home as well as I liked the house on the meadow.

The Feud

One day Dash and I went over the field and walked part way up the big ditch road. When we started back, we met two little girls I didn't know. I said, "Hey ya'll," and they spoke back, and I told them we had recently moved to the new house and didn't know many children. They invited me to their home. We played a while, and then I don't know what happened, but the smaller girl, she was about a year younger than I, fell off of the swing. Her mother ran out, and both girls said I pushed her. I was astonished because I was nowhere near either of them. I was playing with Dash. Suddenly, I felt two very hard slaps across my face and another across my nose, and blood began to flow everywhere. Dash gave one leap and knocked the lady down.

I got off the ground and ran home with Dash. Mama picked me up in her arms. I was all bloody. I told Mama what had happened. I have never seen anything like my mild-mannered Mama when she gets angry, especially when someone harms her children! She took me by the arm and went down to the lady's house. Mama was petite, and this woman was wide and tall. Mama asked her if she was the one that hit me, and the lady said, "Yes, I was, you half-breed mulatto. You keep this black ugly little b—— out of my yard or I'll kick her a— and yours too!" My Mama lit into that woman like a small tornado and beat her up pretty bad! I was crying and Dash was barking to get in the fight. Mr. Anthony came by and pulled them apart, and Mama told her to never put her hands on her children again. She took me home and cleaned me up.

That night, Mr. Anthony came and told us that the woman's husband was going to get Mama back the next day after Papa went to work. My family laughed. They didn't believe a man would dare touch Mama. I saw Charles, Nina, and Odell talking, then they went outside after dark. They came in laughing. We all went to bed that night, and I prayed and asked God to forgive that lady for hitting me, and I asked God to forgive Mama and Dash for hitting that lady.

The next morning I played with knee-baby Nell and baby Vi. We were confined to the porch, which wrapped around two sides of the house. Nina, Charles, and Odell had disappeared right after breakfast. Lucy stayed in her room sewing. She was always sewing.

While playing on the porch, I thought I heard someone laughing, but I thought it was my imagination. After a while, the ice man came by; he stopped in front of our home. He said, "Little girl, is your Mama home?"

I said, "Yasuh."

"Would you call her out for me?"

I called, "Mama!" She came outside wiping her hands on her apron and asked the man what he wanted. He told Mama he had things in the wagon he was selling. Mama went to look in the wagon; the man grabbed Mama by the arm and said, "You hit my wife! Now I'm going to whip the hell out of you!" Mama began to fight him. He took out his horsewhip and began to hit her. After a few seconds, I heard a commotion under the porch and out came Charles, Nina, and Odell. Charles pulled Mama away, her arms flailing the air. Odell and Nina began throwing bricks. Charles came and got a load of bricks, and they hit that man so hard and so many times, people came out of their homes and said, "Hit him! Hit him!" The man ran, leaving his wagon. I saw one of his eyes had been knocked out. He was blind in one eye the rest of his life, I understand.

In all the excitement I threw up. I used to throw up all the time when I became excited. That man was a bloody mess when he left my family, and when Papa came home he was so mad he cried. He and Charles went to the man's house, but they had all gone somewhere and didn't return for quite a while. No one ever bothered us again.

The Farm

There were so many bad things happening on that street. One neighbor came home and found his wife in bed with his best friend. They were both found with their throats slit. I was very sad because I loved that lady. She was always nice to me. Even after a long search, they never found her husband.

Papa told Mama we were going to move somewhere else because this was not a fit place to raise his family. We soon found a very big farm house in Little Washington, a section of Goldsboro near the shopping area. There was plenty of room for Maude and Dash and the children to play. It had a meadow and a creek. The only thing I didn't like was there was a graveyard nearby. On the other side of the graveyard lived Grandma Anna and Grandpa Giles Hicks. To get to their home, you could take a shortcut through the graveyard or go all the way around the road. But the farm was a much better place than the one we had come from.

The next day, which was Saturday, all of the cousins came to see our property, and Papa said he was going to try to buy it so we could have a home for life. My cousin Ervin Sutton, who was the same age as I (about 6 plus), and Uncle Yag's daughter, Sudy, and some others, knee-baby Nell and baby Vi—all went out to play in the yard. It was a very hot day. Ervin went in the house and came out. He said, "Look what I found on the table." It was a plug of tobacco. All the boys chewed, so all of us took some. It tasted awful. The other children asked, "What do you do after you chew it?"

I said, "Swallow it! I'll go in and get a lot of water!"

I went in the house and got a jug already filled with what I thought was water, and I got some tin cups, and I found Mama on the front porch and asked could we have some clabber milk and she came and poured some in the pitcher. I called Ervin to come and help me take it out. We finished chewing and eating the tobacco. We drank the clabber milk, and then we poured all the little tin cups with "water," and it started to take our breath! It tasted awful, so Ervin went inside and got some sugar to put in it, and we all drank it.

Knee-baby Nell was talking to me, and her eyes crossed and she fell back on the ground. One by one, the children began to pass out. Then Ervin and I keeled over. We scared everybody so bad because they couldn't wake us up. They thought we were dead! All of us were drunk, because that jug was filled with white lightning whiskey the brothers had made.

When we came to, hours later, we all vomited tobacco, curdled milk, and whiskey. That was the first and last time that I was ever drunk. The hot sun did not help us any. We were sick for two days! I thought I was going to stay cross-eyed the rest of my life. Ervin and I did not get a whipping, but we received a very stiff lecture. We didn't need a whipping to remember that affair.

Cousin Ervin

Ervin and I had a lot of fun. One day, we put a blanket on Maude and climbed on her back, put the rope on her neck, and started off with Dash following us. We didn't know how to guide a horse, so I just said, "Go Maude!" and Maude went and went! We became tired, but we kept going on and on. Finally, I recognized we were at the property where that white man tried to hurt me. I saw the creek and the railroad. I even tried calling Princess. I saw our old house and the path that lead to the road where Papa went to work.

Ervin and I did not know how to get back home. Thank God for Dash. I said, "Dash, take Maude home." So Dash kept at Maude and brought us to the creek and finally to home. So I realized that the same creek that I played in when we lived on the other property ran near our present property. Everyone was looking for us. You see, we had left that morning, and now Papa was home. When they took us off Maude we couldn't walk; our bottoms were numb! Ervin and I drank nearly all the water out of our well. Maude and Dash drank from the creek. Later on, Papa showed us children how to find spring water if we were ever lost. Ervin and I could not get down off the horse. If we had gotten off, we could not have gotten back on. Papa said, "Why didn't you give the whistle?" But Ervin and I was so scared we forgot to whistle. We did not get punished. They were so happy we were safe. We had to eat standing up, and oh boy, we ate and ate! We were so hungry!

Ervin was spending the week with us even though he lived on the other side of the graveyard. His mother was my first cousin, and he was my second cousin. We were more like brother and sister. We felt much better the next day. We made kites, really good ones and I still can make a mean kite today! My children had the biggest, prettiest kites, and now I am making them for my grandchildren and great-grands. Ervin, knee-baby Nell, and I flew our kites and we had so much fun!

In Town

Ervin and I went exploring one day. We walked so far we saw white children outside playing. I didn't have too much experience with white people. I heard about some awful things that white people did, but I only knew two white men—Mr. Kellog and the man that tried to hurt me. I went up to the little white girl and said, "Hey girl!" She looked me up and down. She came and touched my hair. Mama had wrapped my plaits with white strings. I know I must have been a sight because I was told I wasn't cute at all when I was small. I touched her hair and it was soft and yellow.

Her mother came out of the house and hollered at us. She said, "You little black pickaninnies! Get away from here and go back where you belong!" We ran home crying. That was my first personal encounter with prejudice. I asked Mama what was a black pickaninny? She asked why, and she spanked me and Ervin and told us never to go out of our neighborhood again.

Ervin went home, and I was very lonely. I started going down in the meadows. I would lie down in the grass and read and read. The more I read my Bible, the more I became aware of someone with me in the quiet meadow. I could talk to the animals and birds. I could feel a peace when I was at the creek. I can't explain it, but every time I went to my meadow and creek it seemed as if something special was there. I began to read about Jesus and what He did for me, and when I read how He suffered, I cried so hard. I could really see Him. I didn't know about Him before I received my Bible because the preacher at our other church only preached in the Old Testament. My first Bible became a part of my life.

On Saturday, Papa said we were going into town to shop. We had never gone into town with Mama and Papa before, and it was very exciting. The white people were very mean to Negroes, so Mama and Papa were afraid the family might get into trouble.

Papa gave me ten cents and the older ones twenty-five cents for spending money in town.

We started walking toward the business district. Nina took knee-baby Nell's hand, Lucy took baby Vi's hand, and Papa took mine. As I looked up at Papa, he smiled and gave my hand an extra squeeze. The shop windows were very pretty. There were quite a few colored people out window shopping. They showed us the five-and-ten-cent store. My sisters and brother bought things to eat. I bought a small book for five cents and some lined notebook paper.

On our way home, Papa stopped and bought all of us ice cream. Suddenly, I spied a water spout. I ran up and began drinking. Then a white man and woman cursed at me and called me a "black jigaboo" and told me to get away. I was scared and my Papa came and got me. That was my second encounter with prejudice. I loved everybody, but I was beginning to dislike white people.

The Holy Ghost

After moving, we began going to a new church in town, a Free Will Baptist Church. A lot of our relatives attended. Papa was a deacon; he was in great demand for his beautiful singing. I loved church and was always happy to go.

One Saturday afternoon we went to the home of one of our uncles. We all sat on the porch. Uncle and Auntie brought out cold watermelon, and we ate and talked. There was a large crowd gathering on the corner. People were sitting on steps and on the ground. Some ladies and men were singing hymns and beating tambourines. Everyone was excited.

I got off the porch and inched closer. I saw a woman dressed all in white with white hair standing on the corner. Her beauty nearly took my breath away. She looked like an angel. She began to sing and clap her hands to the music. I began to do the same. When the music stopped, she lifted her hands to Heaven and began to pray. Then she began to preach about something called the Holy Ghost. I was fascinated by her. I had never seen a woman preach. It was the first time I had ever heard about the Holy Ghost. I didn't like the word "ghost," but I felt it was something special.

I noticed people begin to leave. Mama came and took me back to the porch. But I was so interested, that I inched my way back. While the woman was still preaching, I went up to her and touched her dress. I couldn't help myself. I stayed there until she finished. She patted my head and kissed me. I will never forget that episode. It was the first lady preacher I saw and the first time I heard about the Holy Ghost. I remember reading something in my Bible about the Holy Ghost, but I didn't understand it at that time.

After that episode, I would preach to Dash and our horse Maude and all the animals down in my meadow. When I sang to them, Dash would run off!

"Grown"

The seasons came and went. Mama stayed very busy taking care of us, cooking, cleaning, making our clothes. We did a lot of singing at our home. We would all gather around the old piano, which Odell would play, and we all could harmonize a song. Afterward, Mama would serve us homemade root beer and cinnamon cookies or ginger bread.

Sometimes my older brother and sisters would make my parents angry. One day, Charles got smart with Mama. She told him to cut the wood for the stove, and he began to pout. Mama called him, and he turned around very slowly, and quite forcefully she said, "Get that wind out of your jaw and that starch out of your neck!" I was to hear her say that quite a lot as the older ones became what they say is "grown." I realized later that they were in that difficult age of being a teenager. Many a time I saw my little Mama step on the step stool and lay a haymaker with her fist on my brother's chin. They all were taller than Mama, but we all had the utmost respect for her.

In my new neighborhood, I met two little girls who were twins, named Eartha and Earline. They were the same age as I was. I told them we had twins at home, Retha Nell and Letha Bell and a baby sister Vivian Vernell. My new friends were so pretty. At first I was kind of shy around them because I was so homely, but they liked me anyway. We went to the same school and church. Mama liked me to play with them because they were so nice. I took them down to my meadow and showed them my creek, and we would watch the trains go by. Eartha and Earline were a lot of fun to be with.

About three weeks later, I waited for them to come, but they didn't come. After two days, I went by their home. The curtains were closed and no one answered the door. When I went back home, Mama and some neighbors were talking excitedly. I heard Mama say, "I do declare!" She saw me walking so dejectedly she shushed the women up, took me on the porch and asked, "What's wrong, Sugar Pie?"

"Mama, I think maybe I was mean to Eartha and Earline; I don't see them anymore."

"Honey, you are never mean to anyone. Don't ever think that. Sit here beside me. I have something to tell you. Honey, little Earline is dead. God took her."

Well, here we go again, I thought, this mean, bad God was always doing something to hurt and scare me. Oh, how I hated Him.

Mama told me they found Earline dead in her bed. The neighbors heard Eartha crying for so long that they went over and peeked in the curtains. They saw Eartha alone and she told the neighbors that nobody could get up. The neighbors found Earline and her mother dead. I never found out what happened, but my two little friends went out of my life and left quite a void.

My brother and knee-baby Nell and Bell, Nell's twin who died when she was a baby, were very fair-skinned like Ma. Charles was very tall and had what we called good hair like Mama's. He was handsome, and he broke many a lady's heart before he died at forty years of age. Knee-baby Nell was petite like Mama and pretty as a picture. Baby Vi was as cute as a button. She was a grinner and laughed all the time. She was the baby and always got her way; she grew up very spoiled. Nina was tall and thin with hair down to her waist. She was a knockout. She looked more like Papa. All the girls except myself had beautiful dark velvet skin. Lucy was very pretty and not as tall as Nina. She had long pretty hair, and always looked so neat because she made a lot of her clothes. Odell was fair-skinned and tall. She was the nicest and the kindest and the biggest tomboy you would want to see. And then came me. Well, I overheard one of my Aunt's tell Mama that "all the girls were so pretty, but Mog is rather, you know, she's not ugly, but, she's not pretty like the other ones." Then Mama said something I'll never forget: "Mog is the nicest, sweetest child we have. She is very special, and one day people will take notice of Mog in a big way."

I became very shy after hearing my Aunt's remarks, and that's when I began to learn everything by reading everything I got my hands on. I could never hug my Aunt anymore. I became so shy and quiet—an introvert. I was very dark-skinned and my hair was short and thick; I was no beauty. I would look in the mirror and I imagined I saw a monster; her remark really affected me, so even now I become self-conscious thinking about her.

We children played baseball a lot and we would jump rope. I liked making up poetry and songs. I still would walk barefoot through the meadows. I would usually take a book. Most of the time I would read my Bible. I loved lying on my back and looking up at the sky; it was so beautiful, the blue sky and the soft white, cottony clouds. I always felt a special presence when I was there. It seemed as if I were the only one in the world, yet there was always someone else there. I never knew who it was until I grew up and became acquainted with Him. It was Jesus, and He had been protecting me all those years.

One day we all went over to a relative's home to visit. It was always nice when we all got together. I took my book and went out and sat by the side of a tree. I was there for quite a while. My Aunt and my Mama came to look for me. They got near the tree and turned around and ran back screaming for Papa and my uncles. Auntie came running toward me with a great big hoe. Uncle Bud had his rifle and Papa had an ax. Mama ran to the right of me. You can imagine what I thought; they were going to do in this little black ugly duckling! This was it. My heart was pounding so hard. "Why? Why," I thought.

I froze with fright. Mama said real quietly, "Mog Lee, look at me and do everything I tell you to do and do it slowly. You get on your hands and knees and start to crawl toward me very slow, and when I say run, you get up and run!" I did what she said. I dropped my book and slowly got on my knees and started to crawl and when Mama said "RUN!", I started running, and I heard two shots. I didn't look back because I didn't know what they were shooting at. I thought, if they were going to shoot me, they would have to catch me! I ran off down that road, and Charles had to catch me and bring me back. I was so frightened, I didn't know what to do.

Mama, Papa, and all the grownups hugged me. I was so confused. I thought they had all gotten together and decided to shoot me. (I always had a big imagination.) They couldn't stop kissing me. Papa took me over to that tree, and there was the remains of the biggest black snake they had ever seen. He was coiled up like a car tire. I didn't see it when I went out there to read. I almost sat on it, but I didn't. (That was my Lord protecting me.) I have had many a brush with death over the years, but my Lord was always there to protect me. David in his battle with Goliath wasn't the only one who had Goodness and Mercy at his side; they followed me too.

My book was ruined, but Papa said he would get me another one. They told me never to sit near a blackberry field because that is where that snake came from.

Nina was all grown up and very pretty. She had a boyfriend and we really teased her, and she would get angry. The beautiful days went by. I can see all of us together after all these years. Baby Vi with her cute little face, her little skinny legs and three plaits waddling around, following knee-baby Nell. Nell was short and light-skinned like Mama, very quiet, and her hair always was in three braids. They always liked to play with me. We were usually together. Then there is me, tall and skinny, very dark, very thick hair that Mama sometimes wrapped in string or cornrowed. People up north started cornrowing about 1970. We've known about cornrowing all our lives. I was a dreamer and a loner. I liked reasoning things out. I wanted to know the whys and wherefore of things. Then there was Odell. She was very tall and light-skinned and very good looking. She was the kindest and most lovable of my sisters. She was a tomboy, and she would not take anything from anybody and could fight anybody.

Then there was Lucy. She was tall also, very elegant and good looking girl. Her skin was very beautiful. It was between Mama's light skin and Papa's dark skin. She was always very busy doing something with her long hair. Then there was Charles. This guy was the only boy in the family at this time; my older brother had died. Charles was as handsome as any movie star. He was light-skinned, very tall, and liked to dress well. He was quite spoiled and got his way a lot. Those looks of his much later in life were going to cause him a problem. Papa was always counseling him. He was very feisty and would hit you in a minute. Then there was Nina, tall and thin, hair down to her waist. She was a knockout-looking girl. She was just beginning to keep company in the Sunday parlor, and Papa was always nearby cleaning his gun. Papa's gun was to become quite a problem to all of his daughters when we went into our teens.

My Mama didn't weigh more than one hundred twenty pounds, very petite, with beautiful auburn hair down to her waist. She was so very pretty. Papa and all of us adored her. She was as strong as pig iron. Papa was very tall and dignified and handsome. He was gentle with us, but he could be very hard also. Whenever Papa took me in his arms, I felt so safe and secure. I felt nothing could hurt me.

One day, I remember Mama and Papa were talking about me with Aunt Georgianna. Auntie said, "Brother, Mog is a very tender-hearted child. She's going to be hurt in life. She's not strong like your other children. She's going to be persecuted in life, and she's going to be very sickly all her life, but she is going to do some wonderful things in her life. She's going to shed some briny tears and suffer, but she will get through it all right." And those were prophetic words; they all turned out to be true.

There are so many beautiful things I wished I had kept in my mind. So many beautiful moments I wish I could bring back. Well, memory brings its remorse when we recall how blind we were to beautiful things that were so precious, the true value of parents and friends and moments now gone, but so too it has its blessedness when we look back over the journey of life and see how it was divinely planned by the Master Planner.

When playing house with baby Vi and knee-baby Nell, who both had doll babies, I remember regretting that Santa Claus never brought me a doll baby. I made my dolls out of grass and rags. But, by a remarkable coincidence after I was married, my first baby was born on Christmas morning—the most beautiful doll anyone could wish for.

Big Family Day

It was a two-day affair that would start on the last Friday in July and end on Sunday. Our entire family, including my twelve uncles, their wives and children, gathered at Uncle Yag's farm for an enormous party. On Friday, Uncle Lovett would pick close to fifty water melons out of his field and put them in the creek at Uncle Yag's. By Saturday they would be icy cold and sweet.

Papa would fit as many people as he could into his big Franklin car. Uncle Yag would send his big wagon to pick up those along the way who needed rides to the farm. All of the family dogs came as well.

When we got to the last long lane to Uncle Yag's farm, I asked Papa and Mama if I could walk with Dash, and Papa let me out of the car. I liked walking barefoot in the warm sand, carrying my shoes. The wagons would stop, and some of my cousins would get off and walk with me. We would squeal and laugh all the way.

As we got closer to the farm, we could hear laughter. Then the heavenly smell of a barbecue blew down the lane. Three pits would be in use to accommodate our very big family. The yard was filled with relatives, every age you could think of. There were at least six to eleven children my age. We all got together, tossed our shoes in a smelly heap, and ran off to the creek. The earth was warm and soft under our feet. The sun caressed our small brown bodies, and the tall, wheat-like grass tickled our legs.

At the creek we jumped into the shallow water. It was so clear you could see the bottom. The minnows and crawfish swam away from us. We came up on the bank and lay down. After a while, little Willie Rose said, "I'm going to get that pretty kitty cat!" She was four years old, I believe.

Little Willie Rose came and sat down beside us. The cat was all

Willie Rose was soon to get a nickname, (not rose), after finding a black and white "kitty cat." The little ones couldn't run fast enough.

black with a wide, white stripe down its back. Cousin Delmus said, "That kitty cat looks different than our cat." Baby Ray said, "Here's another kitty cat, but it's larger." Then the big cat turned her back, and when Baby Ray went after it, it sprayed us with something that stank so bad we all vomited and started running toward the farm. We were screaming, "Mama, Mama, Mama!!"

About a hundred relatives were running toward us. When we were about five feet from each other, our momentum carried the smell to the grownups. Then they all did the queerest thing, they stopped as if an invisible hand had grabbed them. They turned around and ran away from us as fast as they could. I guess we were a pitiful sight because Mama stopped. I was so happy because I thought she was going to take me in her arms and hug me, but all she did was to hold up her two hands and yell, "STOP!" Then she said, "Baby, go in back of the barn." Now looking back over the years, I can laugh at the picture of it.

I went in back of the barn. There was no one in sight; even the dogs had run away from us! Mama ordered, "Take your clothes off." I was hesitant because I was so modest. As I started to take my clothes off, here came all the mothers with the rest of the little stinkers. We all had to get naked, all eleven of us.

They filled two wooden tubs with water and doused us. Auntie Lou went inside and brought our her rose water and rubbed it on. Then the women took some of Auntie's homespun material and cut seven triangles and fitted us with what looked like diapers. They tied them in the middle, and then made halters for the girls. We were still stinking, so we had to sit off by ourselves to eat and play for the rest of the day. Even our dogs refused to play with us! Uncle Yag and Papa took all of our clothes to the other side of the apple orchard and buried them. Papa came and explained the difference between a cat and a skunk.

Once the three barbecued pigs and food had been eaten, the family played games. The men pitched horseshoes and arm wrestled. The women gossiped, knitted and crocheted, and embroidered. The children played jump rope and hop scotch. We had a potato bag race, and played hide-and-go-seek. After awhile, all of us pitiful little kids in diapers fell asleep on the ground.

Auntie Lou brought out her quilt frame and set it up. All the mothers brought out pieces of cloth from every member of their family. That was in the year 1925. The last time I saw that quilt was in

1962 on a visit to my home in the south. We had gone to Auntie Lou's funeral. She was my favorite aunt.

Oh, how everyone dreaded to see the day come to an end. Everyone began kissing and hugging. We children were kissed rather gingerly, but Mama knew how sensitive I was. She took me in her arms and hugged and kissed me, and that made my day.

Mama, Our Pharmacist

When baby Vi, knee-baby Nell, or I came down with summer colds, Mama got out the sugar and turpentine and we had to take a teaspoonful every few hours. Evidently it did us good because we didn't die. Mama, bless her heart, was a walking pharmacy. Thank God for that! She used to give us sassafras tea she made out of the roots she dug up. In the wintertime when we got chest colds, she would put a piece of flannel in the oven and sprinkle flour on it until the flour browned and she would spray and slap that hot stuff on our chest. We were so glad when we got better because that flour was about to burn us up! When we got fevers, she would slice white potatoes and put them on us until the potatoes got brown. In the Spring, the whole town took sulfur and molasses. That was to clean your system out. When we got chicken pox or measles or any other skin rash, she would go in the field and pick polk leaves and roots. She would boil them and rub us down in it, and we got better. Sometimes she would take and put drops of kerosene on a spoon of sugar and lordy, lordy! We took it! I guess we got better. We are all passed sixty-five years old.

It was almost worth taking that homemade medicine, because afterward, there was always a kiss from Mama. There's only one medicine I never forgave her for giving me, and that was castor oil. She made me take that for a cold until I was sixteen years old, but after that, she would send us to the drug store for Mr. D.B. to mix it with soda. Many a day I brought the soda and pretended that the castor oil did its job. I taught baby Vi and knee-baby Nell to do the same!

All medicines are different now. I believe a lot of the medicine worked because of the love that accompanied it when it was being administered by Mama.

Mama was only a little girl when she left her folks to marry Papa, but she remembered how her Mama took care of the family without a doctor. There were no black doctor's in town, and we only visited a white doctor if there was a serious illness.

God's Wrath

I overheard Papa and his brothers talking about church one day. All of Papa's brothers were deacons. It seemed as if some of the congregation wanted to get rid of the pastor because a certain woman claimed she had something going on with the Reverend. Uncle Bud said the woman was a liar because she lied about all the men she couldn't get. Papa said, "They are not getting rid of Rev."

You see, my grandparents had originally founded the church under a mulberry bush along with my aunt, Papa's sister, and older brothers, and my parents felt they would have some say in the matter. A meeting was held and some said Reverend had to go, but my Papa stood up and told them he didn't want the church split. He didn't believe in confusion. He said it was not true what the woman said. "I forgive her," he said. "God would speak for him and let the people know she lied." When he left he told them he loved them and that God would have mercy on their souls.

A few days later there was a very bad thunderstorm. As a six-year old, I was very scared of thunder and lightning because some older children told me that when there was a storm God was angry with everyone. He was pushing furniture around, and He was going to push it over onto our heads. And when it was lightning God was whipping someone. Papa and Mama would make us sit still, and they would pray to God not to harm the family. I felt God was cruel. Between my former pastor preaching hell and damnation and the older children telling me all that junk, I was a basket case during a storm.

On this particular day, God was pushing the furniture around in a rage. It rained, thundered, and lightninged like never before. After a while, there were two or three sharp cracks and then we heard people screaming, "No, God! No, God!" I wondered what God had gone and done now. Hadn't He done enough? I thought the people screaming were being hit with the furniture God was throwing. Papa ran outside. I didn't expect to see him again.

Papa was gone for a while. Then he burst through the door. "Mama! Mama!" he cried, "God has struck the church and it's on fire!"

Everyone raced outside. It was still raining, but all the noise had stopped. I couldn't move because I had wet myself from fear. I was petrified. I never told my family how I felt. I was crying so hard because everyone else was crying. I covered my face with my hands.

I finally went outside, and I got wet from the rain. Now no one could tease me about what happened. All the grownups were crying and moaning and saying God was showing the people they didn't treat the Reverend right. Free Will Baptist burned down to the ground. I can imagine there were a lot of people repenting.

The next few days were full of activity. We spent most free time at the church site. I sat under the chinaball tree with knee-baby Nell and baby Vi while the family raked the rubbish away. Church was held in various homes.

The church wasn't rebuilt immediately. When they began, the entire family helped. I carried one brick at a time. Finally it was finished. It was a beautiful brick church. Whenever I visit down south, I feel a sense of pride when I look upon this house of God I helped create over sixty-five years ago.

The first Sunday we marched into the new church I will never forget. The entire congregation wore white, children and grownups alike. The old minister was called upon, but he would not come back. I don't blame him. The new minister was a relative of ours and a very good preacher. He visited us a lot. Papa and his brothers sang and what a group of singers they were! One of our female relatives played the piano. There was a lot of food that we ate outside. It was one of the happiest days of my life.

The Graveyard

One early evening, Mama told Odell and Lucy to go over Grandma's to borrow some kerosene. I asked Mama if I could go too. The girls said, "No!" But Mama allowed me to go along. Odell and Lucy got the kerosene can, but they forgot to put the top on. They said, "Let's go through the graveyard. It's shorter and we can stay longer."

I didn't want to go through the graveyard. I heard there were haints in there. But my sisters would not listen to my fears, and with quaking knees, we entered the path through the graveyard. We began to trot, and with each step we heard a thin "Whooo!" sound very close. We began to run. When we stopped to catch our breath, the "whooing" stopped. After we rested, we started running again, and that "whooing" kept on until we stumbled into Grandma's. We couldn't talk. I had wet myself from fright.

My sisters told Grandma Anna what had happened. We told her a haint had chased us. She said, "There is no such thing as haints." Yes there is, I thought. Who does she think she's kidding? Grandma filled the can and asked for the cap. They told her they didn't have it. She burst out laughing and told us that air had gotten into the spout when we ran and made that "whooing"! We were relieved.

While we were at Grandma's, she gave us some sarsaparilla and cinnamon crisps. While my sisters were eating, I went in to use the commode, and there were four pennies on Grandma's chifferobe. I quickly snatched them. I don't know why. I hadn't seen too much money before. I couldn't remember seeing so many pennies.

My sisters called me and I came out of the commode with the four pennies in my hot palm. We kissed Grandma goodbye. It took us a long time to get home, because we decided to go around the big road instead of cutting through the graveyard. It was beginning to turn gray outside, and my legs were growing tired. I was glad we got home before dark.

Well, I have had three heart attacks in my life, and I think what happened after I got home from Grandma's was the beginning of them. I dropped a penny on the wooden floor. Mama asked, "What was that?" She stooped and picked it up, saying "Oh! Grandma gave you all pennies!"

Odell and Lucy shook their heads and said, "No."

Mama turned to me smiling, "Grandma give you a penny?"

"No, Mama" I said.

"Where did you get this penny, honey?"

"Mama, they were on Grandma's chifferobe and I picked them up," I said, smiling.

Mama said, "What is that you are holding?"

I opened my hand. Mama took the three other pennies and asked if Grandma knew I had them.

"No, Mama."

"Well Mog, you are going to take them back to Grandma tonight and you are going through the graveyard."

My breath nearly stopped.

"But Mama, it's dark and I can't see the path!"

"The moon is shining and you can see the path!" Mama took me to the door and said, "Go now, and come right back!"

When I got to the path I ran as fast I could. I heard something, in back of me but didn't dare turn around. I thought a haint was try-

41

ing to catch me. I found out later that Mama had secretly sent Charles to follow me.

I fell through Grandma's door and into her arms. She had to hold me tight because my heart was pounding so. I was crying hard and I told her I had taken her pennies. I was sorry. I didn't mean to be bad. I was sobbing because I didn't want to go back through the graveyard. Grandma went most of the way with me. I was somewhat numb when I got home. Mama talked to me about taking something that didn't belong to me. She didn't have to worry because I never did it again. I was restricted to the house. I couldn't play with Dash or Maude. I couldn't go to my creek and meadow. I was really miserable.

Baptism

Papa told Mama that the church was going to baptize after morning church on Sunday. Papa said Nina, Lucy, Charles, and Odell would be baptized. Papa told them about something called repenting and he prayed with them.

After one Sunday service the Pastor led the town on a grand march to the nearby river. Several teenagers in the congregation were going to be baptized. They were dressed in white robes and went barefoot. The Pastor stood in the water, cradled each person in his arms and dunked them. He was doing real well until he got to the twelfth young man. When he got ready to baptize him, the Pastor went down also! We kids laughed. I heard the other members of my family laughing about it when we got home. It was a beautiful time. Little did I know those long, lazy days were coming to an end.

The next day, cousin Ervin came to the house with his mother. We got on Maude and rode around the meadow, then went home for lunch. After lunch, Mama told me to play with knee-baby Nell and baby Vi. Ervin and I and some other young relatives went down to the creek. We all sat around. We were talking about the baptism. There were about seven of us, and we were all under seven years old. Ervin said, "Let's baptize in the creek."

It seemed like a good idea. I told the children about "pentin'" of their sins. I told them we were going to wash their sins away. We sang "Take Me to the River".

Ervin and I put all the children in the creek. We were supposed to baptize Dash, but he ran away. I had knee-baby Nell and baby Vi. We put them face down in the creek and screamed, "Pent! Pent!" We were trying to say "repent." The water wasn't deep. It covered their little bodies. We kept them in the water; they were kicking.

Finally, Ervin and I pulled them out and laid them on the grass. They did not move. I kept shaking them. We became frightened. "They're dead!" I said.

Ervin said, "We will have to bury them! We don't have anything to dig a grave with. I'll sneak to the house and get Uncle's shovel."

I was so scared. I didn't know what to do. While Ervin was away, the children began coughing. Boy, was I glad to hear all of them coughing! Then they all sat up.

In the meantime, Ervin was caught with the shovel. Uncle Bud asked him what he was doing and where were all the children. He burst out crying and said we had drowned them. Uncle Bud hollered to the family and about twenty of them went tearing through my meadow. Oh! The look on their faces when they saw everybody was safe.

They took us all to the house. Little did I know what was ahead for me. All the cousins went home. Cousin Clara took Ervin to the woodshed. I heard him crying. Mom had a smile on her face. She told me to come into the room and talk. I eventually learned that when that particular smile was on Mama's face and she said "lets talk in the room," that someone's backside was going to be acquainted with the leather strap. This was the first time I had been beaten with the strap. Up till then I had received a little love spanking when I misbehaved. What that little woman did to my legs and my bottom! All the time she was whipping me, she repeated, "I love you." Now, this I didn't understand. She beat me until I wet myself. I was in shock. Then she had the nerve to take me in her arms and hug me and tell me she loved me. I didn't believe her. I really thought she beat me so hard because I was ugly, not pretty like the rest of the family. From that day on, I had a very healthy respect for that leather strap.

I have seen the strap wreak vengeance on my brother and sisters many a day. We used to get what I later called "wholesale beatings." Usually if someone broke a vase or a lamp chimney or something and refused to admit it, then Mama made everyone but Nina line up by age. If the older ones did something wrong, no one would dare squeal on them because they would make your life miserable. Mom would whip us down the line. I was usually the middle one and by the time she got to me, she was really wound up. She could really lay leather to the hide, while I think Papa was too chicken to lick girls.

One day, Papa came home while Mama was doing a wholesale whipping. He looked at me. I guess he felt sorry for me. I was really a basket case by then. He said, "Mama, I'll help you. I'll take Mog in the other room and whip her."

He began to take his belt off. "Oh God," I thought. I thought he loved me, but now he is going to try to kill me."

Papa took me into the room and closed the door. He raised the strap. I closed my eyes and let out a scream, but I didn't feel a thing. Papa said, "Scream!" but every time the belt came down I didn't feel anything, so by then I thought I must be dead. Finally he stopped, and I saw Papa had been hitting the pillow. He was crying when he hugged me and said out loud,"I whipped you because I love you."

Knee-baby Nell and baby Vi were the last ones I baptized, even after I became a minister forty years later.

The Disappearances

The beautiful days went by. Quite a few of our relatives became hunted by the KKK. Some were beaten; a few were lynched. Everyone was becoming quite angry at the segregation and Jim Crow practices. Mama and Papa did not take us uptown very much because the white people made Papa so angry, and my brother had become so reckless he was always challenging some white person. In our schools, we were taught to be proud of our race, and we were taught about slavery and all about our famous black people. I became very interested in them, and that interest prevails today.

One Saturday, a big cookout was held at Uncle Yag's farm. Like most of the family barbecues it was filled with delicious food, games, and the good spirit of relatives and friends. It was to be the last time we would be together with so much love and fun. Sunday was another beautiful day, the sun was shining brightly. We all sat down together and had a big beautiful breakfast. Papa and Mama prayed. We told God how much we thanked Him. We all were dressed so pretty in our starched dresses and black patent leather shoes, our hair braided so nice. Mama and Papa looked so good. The service at the church was nice. Everyone told Mama and Papa what a nice family they had. After church, we walked slowly home. We had to stay dressed up. We were not allowed to play on Sunday. Company came in the afternoon. The grownups sat on the porch and talked. We children walked around and talked. Mama served food. We all had a lot of fun. That was to be our last Sunday with the relatives and going to Free Will Baptist Church with all the family.

The very next day I got out of bed early so I could eat with Papa. He let me sip his coffee from his saucer and dunk my biscuit. I walked part way down the road with Papa. Little did I know that it was to be my last walk down that dusty road with him. Had I known the forthcoming events, I probably would have died. I don't think my heart could have taken it.

Mama had started her wash. The older children went off to farmer Kellog's, while baby Vi and knee-baby Nell were fed breakfast. I played with Dash while Mama hung out her wash. She used bluing in her wash and had the whitest clothes I have ever seen. With such a big family, she was justly proud that our clothes were always white.

Mama usually washed and ironed on Monday in the afternoon. Mama had made a fire in the little parlor stove to heat the flat irons on. It was summertime and very hot. She had the ironing board put in place. She had sprinkled her clothes and was waiting for the flat irons to heat. She had pulled her dress off and was down to her slip because of the stifling weather. She often did that when it was hot. Baby Vi and knee-baby Nell and I were playing on the floor in the same room. We had put Dash outside because he wasn't allowed in the parlor.

Mama began ironing. The door opened and, without knocking, the white insurance man walked in. You see, we never locked doors. Mama tried to cover herself. We stared at the man with apprehension. Mama put Papa's shirt in front of her. The white man snatched the shirt from Mama and said, "You sure are a pretty nigga woman." He patted Mom on her backside. Mama reached over and picked up the iron on the stove and slapped it across his cheek. I can still hear his skin sizzling. He started screaming and slapped Mama in the face. You could see the mark of his hands on her pretty face. We children started crying. He drew back to hit her again, and she hit his hands with the iron. He called her a terrible name and said he was going to get her.

My brother and sisters came home. They all wanted to go find the man, but Mama wouldn't let them. When Papa found out what had happened he was so angry that he cried. He and Mama went to the bedroom and talked. The older girls fixed our supper, and I wondered why white people were so mean. We weren't slaves, and they seemed to hate us because of our color. I have since hoped they would be forgiven.

After it started getting dark, Papa went out. He and Charles gave the special whistle in every direction. In about an hour, all eleven uncles, along with their older sons came to our house. They had a conference in the backyard, and later returned. We didn't sleep well, and all through the night Papa and Mama came in to kiss and hug us. Papa was crying. I was very scared.

The next day I missed eating with Papa; he went on to work. All the older children stayed home. Charles had Papa's gun. There were baseball bats placed in different areas of the house. There was boiling water, cans of lye, and sharp knives hidden out of sight. I didn't know what was going on. Dash was placed at the front door along with two axes. Papa's nephews were hiding in the meadow. We three children were taken next door. My family thought the white man was coming back to carry out his threat, and we were ready to die or kill in defense of Mama. He didn't come back that day, but the family stayed on the alert.

Mama put us to bed. I heard her moving busily about the house, but I couldn't see what she was doing. I felt something important was going on. There were no lamps lit. Papa came in through the back door. I could hear my parent's whispering. Then they came into our bedroom. Papa took each of us in his arms. Nell and Vi were asleep, but I was pretending. He took me in his arms and hugged me tight and kissed me. He was crying. Then he got up softly in the dark and closed the door. That was the last I would see of my Papa for two years. I didn't know what was going on. I cried all night.

The next morning I got up early so I could eat with Papa. I ran to the kitchen. Mama was cooking. I asked her, "Where is Papa?"

She wouldn't look at me. She said, "He's gone."

I thought she meant he had gone to work. I ran out to the yard to call him, but the road was empty. I went back in the house.

"I'll see him when he comes home," I said.

My brother and older sisters got up. They were so quiet. It was unusual for them to be quiet, they were always joking and teasing and hitting one another, but this morning they gave off an air of sadness. Baby Vi and Nell came in to the kitchen rubbing their eyes. Mama hugged them, and Odell and Lucy fed them. No one went to Mr. Kellog's that day.

I took Dash and went down to my meadow. I put my feet in the creek. I laid in the grass and cried. I didn't know why, but I couldn't stop. I started to talk to that presence that was usually with me. I poured out my heart to whomever it was. Then I fell asleep and woke to Dash licking my face. Auntie Lou came to visit Mama, and they went out and sat under the tree to talk. I saw them crying in each other's arms.

Later on, Dash and I went down the road to wait for Papa to come home. [I can still see that little girl and that dog waiting in the road for her Papa. What a pitiful sight they made.]

Charles took me back to the house. We sat down to eat. I asked Mama, "Where's Papa? I want to wait and eat with him."

The older ones went outside. They were crying. Mama sat down and said, "The train took Papa away, but you will see him soon." I didn't say anything. I went out the door and ran through the meadow. I could hear the train's whistle approaching down the track. I thought is was coming to bring my Papa home, but the wheels never stopped, and the train passed over the trestle. My heart sank and I sat down and cried.

And then, that night, what every Negro in the South dreaded finally happened. About eight men burst into our house. They wore white hoods with eyes cut out. They were very rough. The house was illuminated by their torches. We could see them as they searched for Papa. Charles, Nina, Lucy, and Odell wanted to light into them, but Mama made them stop. They told Mama they would burn down the house and flush Papa out. Charles said, "We thought the KKK had him!" They searched some more, then finally left. My heart had nearly stopped. I was so scared. Baby Vi and knee-baby Nell's little eyes were so big. They were trembling. I remember thinking, "No one should frighten you like this."

Three or four of my uncles began to disappear. They had defended themselves or their family against the white man. Every time a Negro was beaten or hung, you would hear of one or two whites being beaten badly. I found out after I grew up some why Papa had disappeared. After that white insurance man patted Mama and slapped her, Papa and his brothers got someone to trick him in a car. They tied and blindfolded him and took him down to Froggie Bottom and put a hurting on him that he never recovered from. He was found two days later. That's why the KKK came into our home. They went to our neighbor's homes looking for Papa. They went to his brothers' homes as well. I didn't know where Papa was. All I knew was that a train had taken him away. Every day I went to the trestle and waited, but nothing happened. I was so lonely for my Papa.

47

And then one morning Charles disappeared. I learned that he and some local boys went through town and tore down the "For White" and "For Colored" signs. They broke windows and did a lot of damage. They beat up some white boys. After years of suffering at the white man's hand, the blacks had declared war. In fear for his life, Charles disappeared. My sisters and I went to school and existed, but I was confused and frightened. There were forces pulling my family apart, and I was helpless to prevent it.

It was a frightful summer and fall. The holidays brought no relief from our fears. Then, Odell and Lucy disappeared. What's going on? It got to the point where I was afraid to let anyone out of my sight. But the inevitable happened. I don't know how it happened. Baby Vi and knee-baby Nell and I were put to bed one night. Mama and Nina stayed up late.

The next morning, there was no one in the house but Nina and I. "Where's Mama and Nell and Vi," I asked Nina?

"Mog, come here." She took me in her arms and told me the train took Mama and baby Vi and knee-baby Nell away.

"Not again! I can't take anymore!" I was too stunned to cry. I sat in the house afraid to let Nina out of my sight. I was scared to go to school. I became withdrawn. If that wasn't bad enough, my cousin came crying to our home to tell us Ervin had died last night. He had been bitten by a black cat the week before, and it poisoned him and he died. The feeling of remorse was so strong I didn't want to live.

I went down to my meadow and left Nina and my cousin crying. I lay in the grass and I began to think over everything that had been happening. I came to the foolish conclusion that this was Mama and Papa's way of getting rid of me. I knew that one day I would wake up and be alone, that my entire family would abandon me. It was more than I could handle. I climbed up to the train tracks and started walking. There was no sense in going on. I was going to walk until the train hit and killed me. When I got to the trestle I looked down. I was so scared that I froze, all my muscles locked up. I heard Dash barking and it snapped me back to reality. Trembling, I crawled back off the trestle. I wanted to live, even though I thought I was ugly and nobody wanted me. I thank God today that my angels were there protecting me.

Those were dark days. I didn't understand death. Cousin Ervin was so young. And I didn't know how resourceful my family really was. Nina was like a mother to me. I didn't know the need for secrecy.

Reunited

After Ervin's funeral, Nina told me that we were going to move to Uncle Yag's farm. I didn't want to leave my meadow and creek, but, at seven years old, I didn't have a say in the matter. Why couldn't they see what they were doing to me?

We moved away from our friends, and we gave all the furniture away. We took our clothes and the family Bible, my books, Dash and Maude, and moved to Uncle Yag's farm. Every waking hour, I turned to reading and doing school work. Maude broke her leg. Uncle tried to fix it, but it wouldn't heal, and after a few days, Uncle Yag took her somewhere while I was at school and shot her. Now something else I loved was taken from me.

The days went numbingly by. Christmas at the farm was lonely. I didn't receive much for Christmas. Many times I walked the acres of the farm. I kept waiting for Nina to disappear. At night I would hear the mournful whistle of the train, and it would break my heart. I cried every time I heard a train whistle. I am affected by the sound to this day.

One day, Nina received a letter that made her very happy. There was a lot of money in it. She picked me up and danced around and asked me if I wanted to go on a long trip on a train. I had mixed feelings. I didn't know what to expect.

On the tenth of July, 1929, Uncle Yag and Auntie packed fried chicken, biscuits, and cake and put us on the train. We rode all night. I was so nervous. I didn't know where we were going. I fidgeted all evening and could only manage a few hours sleep.

We awoke and ate, and I stared through the train window at the passing landscape. Everything appeared enormous. I saw more cars than I had every seen before. I saw farms and mountains, people and factories. I fell asleep and was awakened by Nina offering me another chicken sandwich, but I was too nervous to eat.

The conductor came through the train and said, "We will arrive at Thirtieth Street Station in twenty minutes." Nina washed my face and hands and smoothed out my pongee dress. I had on white stockings and black patent leather shoes. She combed my hair and tied a ribbon in it, and she fixed the big sash and bow on my dress.

We were both very excited. "Thirtieth Streeeet Staaatioon!" called out the conductor. "We are coming into Thirtieth Street Station. Keep your seats until we come to a complete stop!" I was so nervous I was ready to throw up. I didn't know where we were going. Nina hadn't told me anything. "We are at Thirtieth Street Station! Thirtieth Streeet Staaatiooon!"

The train halted with a jerk, and then came to a grinding stop. Nina took our bags, and we got in a moving line. I clung to the back of my sister's skirt, terrified that I would lose her. Nina got off first, and when I finally stepped down, there were two pairs of outstretched arms waiting to receive me. I thought I had died and gone to Heaven. There stood Mama and Papa. I jumped into their arms and kissed and hugged them. I was crying so hard. I thought I would never see them again. It had been two years since I had seen Papa and about a year and a half since I had seen Mama, my sisters, and brother. My Mama's sister was there as well. I was so excited, I would not let go of Mama and Papa's hands. My world had been restored. I thought about my dog Dash and I hoped Auntie would take good care of him back on the farm.

The family piled into two cars and we drove for a long time. We finally pulled up to a large brick house with a yard. The street and sidewalk were made of cement, unlike the dirt paths I was used to back home. There was a big factory across the street. A big dog came running up to the car when we got out. His name was J.B., and he belonged to my aunt. We were to become inseparable friends.

I held on to Papa's hand as he showed me the house and yard. I was bewildered to find that my aunt was the only Negro on the block. I told Mama I had to go to the outhouse. She took me to a room in the house with pretty flowers on the wall. It had a toilet and a long tub, a cabinet and mirror, and hot and cold running water. It didn't have Orphan Annie comics papering the walls like we had down home. This was the first indoor bathroom I ever saw.

My aunt had married a very rich man, and was nice enough to take our family into her home until we could find a place of our own. We occupied three rooms on the third floor. It was nice, but rather cramped. My aunt had a woman who worked for her, Miss Ethel, who prepared the meals on a big black and white stove. The stove was electric, unlike the one at home.

Our town was called Riverside, New Jersey. The date was July 11th, 1929—and I was eight years old.

Part Two

Up North

My first days in Riverside were bewildering. Brick buildings, roads and sidewalks, white people living on both sides of my aunt's house: I didn't know if I belonged, but I was with Papa and Mama again. It was summer and there was no school, but we all rose early. I would go outside in the yard while Miss Ethel fixed our breakfast. I later learned that Mama did not like this; she wanted to do her own cooking. In the yard I was approached by two little white girls with blonde hair. They spoke to me, but I didn't know whether to answer them or not. I didn't want any problems. I finally said, "Hey!" and ran into the house. They came into the house and spoke to everyone. I hid behind Mama's skirt. Auntie came and took me by the hand and introduced me to Mildred and Ruthie. That was my first encounter with kind, good-hearted white people. They ate breakfast with us and afterward took me on a tour of the block. We were the only blacks in the neighborhood.

Neighborhood

There was a park nearby and a school. In fact, there were two schools. I thought I was going to go to school with Mildred and Ruthie, but I had to walk three miles from our home to get to school. Segregation was just as bad up North as it was in the South. We had to pass my new school to get to our church, First Baptist, in Riverside. Papa became a deacon. Mama was on the Mothers' Board. My older sisters and brother joined the choir. It was a pleasant summer, much nicer than the last two I had spent down South.

We lived in a small neighborhood with the streets named after the presidents. In that neighborhood were Polish, Italian, Japanese, Lithuanians, Chinese, Dutch, Jamaicans, and Negroes. I had so many girlfriends. We were at each other's homes all the time. We played games, we ran races, played double Dutch and mumbly peg. I taught them how to play baseball and skin the cat. I learned to talk some Polish and Italian. I could talk with a Jamaican dialect. I learned to do a lot of exploring and I found a small patch of grass near a sewer plant where I could sit and read and dream of my meadow back home and Dash, long since dead.

Papa got a job in a factory, the Riveredge Metal Company, and eventually found us a home not too far from Auntie's. It was across the street from our cousins and next door to my teacher-to-be. It wasn't as large as our other homes, but it had a sizable yard to play in. After we were settled, the teacher came and introduced herself. Her name was Miss Tannery, and I liked her a lot. She came with her mother and brought a big chocolate cake. She was one of two teachers that taught grades first through eighth. Charles and Nina had quit school and had gotten jobs. Lucy, Odell, Nell, and I went to our new school. Nell and I were in one room, and Lucy and Odell were in another.

On the fifth day, Miss Tannery, after giving me a test, asked Mama and Papa if she could place me in a grade higher because I was capable of doing the work. They agreed and I was placed in a higher grade, worked very hard, and did well. I wanted to be on the honor roll every month. All through elementary school, I made the honor roll with straight As and Bs.

But the children made fun of our heavy southern accent, and I didn't like that. They laughed at us. Along with the dresses that Mama made for us, we wore striped bloomers. As the winters were colder up North than down South, Mama made us wear long drawers. We had to put the legs of the long drawers down in our long stockings. Then our striped bloomers were put on over our long drawers. The children began to call us "baseball drawers." It was very embarrassing. I tried ignoring it, but Lucy, Odell, and even Nell would start swinging fists until they stopped. Mama always packed our lunches in little tin buckets. She would pack us collard greens, ham hocks, rice or lima beans, black-eyed peas, corn bread, or fried fish and potato biscuits. Every day it was something different. Sometimes when the weather was good, Mama would walk three miles one way to bring us hot lunches. When we saw the other children eating sandwiches and pop, we became ashamed and we would go and hide and eat. But, at recess, my sisters and I excelled in baseball, dodge ball, and kick ball.

Everyone wanted us on their team. Down home we started playing hard ball as soon as we could throw.

I was doing well at school. I won several spelling bees and always made excellent grades. I really liked my teacher. I was still self-conscious about my homeliness, and Mrs. Tannery noticed it. I told her what I heard my aunt saying one day about my being really homely. She told me to wait a few years and see what was going to happen. I was nice and tall and thin, she said, and if I stayed good, one day my goodness would show through.

Odell, Nell, and I started going home across the field. It was near the high school where the big kids went. Two great big boys who were in high school would pass us every day. They would make fun of us. They were Negro boys. They yanked Odell's hair one day, and she and feisty Nell started swinging fists and throwing books. I tried to make peace and reason with them to stop fighting, and when they wouldn't stop, I would take off for home to get Charles or Papa. Many a day I tried to stop them fighting, but I couldn't. I had the fightingest sisters you have ever seen. Even baby Vi grew up fighting beside them. I was always trying to make peace. Sometimes they would be ragged when they got home from school. I never got a wrinkle. Odell said, "Mog won't stay and help us fight." I told Mama the girls didn't have to answer the boys back, but no, the girls gave back word for word and ended up fighting. Mama said maybe they should do like I did. To date, I am over seventy years old, and have never been in a fight, and I'm no coward.

My sisters kept fighting with those two boys. After I grew up, those same two boys asked me to marry them. Later on in the years, those boys and my sisters became good friends.

There was a house near school that had a fence around it and a bush in the front yard. Many a day I hid behind that bush and ate my lunch. One day, this very pretty lady came out and began to talk to me. She was a Negro woman, for our school was in a Negro neighborhood. Her name was Mrs. Jenny Jamison, and she was very friendly. I told her I was sorry, I wouldn't sit under her bush again. She said, "It's all right. Come anytime." She asked me why I didn't eat at school, and I told her about the children laughing at our clothes, the way we talked, and our lunches. She told me to come into the house anytime I wanted to and eat my lunch at her kitchen table. Eventually, Mrs. Jenny Jamison became a very big influence in my Christian life.

A Good Christian

A few days later, during lunch break, I went into Mrs. Jamison's house. Inside, I felt a strong presence, the same feeling I got when I went down to my meadow and read my Bible. It was the kind of warmth that made you feel happy and safe. As I began to lose my shyness with her, she asked me if I had a Bible. I told her yes.

She said, "Always keep your Bible at hand. Read it all the time. I have a Bible for you that you can keep here."

After lunch, she began to read the Bible with me and to teach me. She taught me about Jesus and how he died and sent the "Holy Ghost." She began to introduce me to the good God and not to the one I conceived of as a child—the cruel God I despised. I never told Mama and Papa about my innermost feelings of hate for that mean God. But Mrs. Jamison set me straight, and opened up a whole new world to me.

I am so glad that I learned all about God from Mrs. Jamison. I learned that He was a God of love and compassion. He was a God of long suffering. I learned that He had only one Son, and that He sent His only Son down here just to see about me because He loved me. How different this was from the vengeful God of thunderbolts and lightning that I knew as a child. In later years, when my own children were small, I was careful to explain to them the natural phenomena of thunder and lightning.

I visited Mrs. Jamison at lunchtime often. She would read me passages of the Bible and then explain them to me, and she told me about the Holy Ghost again. I wasn't afraid of the word "ghost" now. After we read the Bible, she prayed for me. One day at Mrs. Jamison's, I fainted; I don't know or understand what happened. When I came to, I was crying very hard, but I felt wonderful and happy. I didn't realize how late it was. I didn't go back to school after lunch, but had stayed at Mrs. Jenny's house all afternoon. The teacher got in her car and went to my house to see if I went home. She brought Mama and Charles back. They were looking all over for me.

When they found me about 4:30PM, I was walking across the field instead of going around the road to get home. Mama hugged me so tight. She and Mrs. Tannery asked me where had I been all day? All I could do was cry and say, "I love you Mama," and hug her back.

They took me home and kept asking, "Did anything bad happen?" They thought maybe I had had the same experience when the man tried to hurt me down in the meadow. They were relieved when I told them I was fine.

"Well, where were you?" Mama insisted.

I finally told them I was at Mrs. Jamison's house. Well, you may have thought I told them I killed somebody! All the ladies were saying, "Lawd have Mercy! My God! My God! Saints preserve us! Lawd, we're asking for Your Mercy. Mrs. Jamison's got that Holy Ghost. She's crazy!" They shook me and said, "Don't ever go there again! She's bewitched and crazy! She'll make you crazy if you go there again!" Well, I couldn't be any crazier than I was at that minute. Those ladies had me so scared, shaking me and scolding me, I began babbling and talking strangely.

They took me to Dr. Cannery. He gave me some bitter medicine. The Jamaican lady came over and said I was hexed. Oh! My Lord! Ignorance is terrible. I learned later on that none of those women knew the Bible. If they knew the word of God they would have realized what had happened to me. I had been baptized in the Holy Spirit at the age of nine.

Mrs. Jamison was a beautiful woman filled with the spirit of the Holy Ghost. She had been ostracized and talked about and attended church in Camden. But, Mama just went along with the other ladies.

One day at lunch, I went past Mrs. Jamison's house. It had been over a month since that incident. When I saw her looking out her window, I threw a note in her yard. I explained why I couldn't come to her house anymore. I knew my teacher and sisters were watching me. About two days later, she wrote me a note and told me to look under her bush. In a letter she encouraged me to keep reading my Bible, which I did. I had no contact with her for a long time after that. I was only nine years old; I had to obey my elders. But, she came to me later when I needed her. With the Holy Spirit, Mrs. Jamison saved my life.

Nurturing Spirit and Soul

We played a lot that first summer in the North. We did a lot of exploring with all the children of different nationalities. I decided after learning some Polish I would start on Chinese. I soon became bored with that. I started writing short stories and poems. Here is a poem I made up in the summer of my tenth year:

I Wonder - By Margaret Hicks

Where do the birds go
When the nighttime comes?
When the gray skies
And cottony clouds
Swallow the setting sun.
Then black as coal
Comes the mystery that's night
With all its strange noises
It brings out all my fright.

So I climb on my stool
Pull the covers over my head
And soon I find myself
Asleep in my bed.

One Saturday afternoon I called all the children in the neighborhood together. I put a table in the yard and took Mama's white sheet and made a robe for myself. I stood in the yard and began to preach about the "Sermon on the Mount." Cars began to stop and people, white and Negro, came into the yard. All that teaching Mrs. Jamison gave me was coming on strong. I kept on and on. There was a Catholic priest living two blocks down from us, and he came to see what was going on. He was there when Mama and Papa came home. I was winding down by then. Mama and Papa took me in the house. Father Flint knocked on the door, and Papa let him in. He asked Mama who taught me the Bible, and Mama said, "She taught herself." Father Flint said it had to come from God because the gift that I displayed was rare. He told them to be careful and watch over me because God had his hands on me. I was crying so hard I couldn't stop. I was so confused inside. What was happening to me? Father Flint told me I was going to shed some tears in my lifetime.

Soon winter was here, bringing ice skating on a man-made pond and sliding down Jefferson Hill. We loved playing in the snow. We would build gigantic snow men and hollow them out. We would put them on corners and out in front of neighbors' homes. When people passed, we would stick our arms out of the holes and tip our hats and speak to them. We frightened many people.

It didn't matter how much it snowed, our school was always

open. A distant relative attended school with us. We called her Fish, and she became a friend for life. Fish and I worked to get a perfect attendance award. We found school a great challenge and didn't let anything stop us from getting there. We had to walk six miles round trip. When we got to school, our teacher would bring out a large bottle of cod liver oil and make us down a tablespoonful, followed by two saltine crackers. How we hated cod liver oil!

Our black teachers did not let us get away with anything. They made sure we understood our lessons before we went home. We were getting to the age when we were noticing boys and they were watching us. There was one boy who liked me, Jimmy Henderson. He stole all of his Mother's beautiful handkerchiefs and scarves and gave them to me! I developed a love for beautiful handkerchiefs that prevails today. Another boy, B.J., wrote me a note and asked me to marry him. We were in the fifth grade at the time. We told each other we would love each other until we died.

One day, my teacher asked me what I wanted to be when I grew up. I said, "Anything!" When she heard that, she hit the ceiling. She told me I was college material, and I could reach the top if I kept working hard. She began to work with me toward that goal, and encouraged me to continue to study and learn.

Things were getting rough for my parents. Papa was told he would soon be laid off from his job. My parents were very worried. We didn't have a large garden in the summer or chickens and pigs like we had in the South. But Papa was very resourceful and found temporary work to keep food on the table.

Learning to Swim—The Hard Way

For Easter, Mama and Papa usually outfitted two of us each year with a coat, dress, shoes, and a hat. This year it was my turn. Mama bought me a sky blue coat, blue hat, white dress and shoes. My sister Nell and Vi and all of our friends had been to morning services at church. I was so proud of my blue outfit. I even had white gloves and a white purse.

After church, our gang decided to look for violets. The flowers were plentiful, and we tried to see who could find and make the biggest bunch. Our gang was made up of Fish, Bossy, Nell, Vi, Bob, Jack, Joe, and Maggie. All of us were really dressed nice. Someone suggested we go down to the field by the sewage plant. We all went.

We came to some large rocks that were built over the sewage waste. The waste dumped into the Delaware River. Someone spied all of those beautiful violets on the other side. Two of the children went over, and then I went. Little Joe was afraid to walk on the rocks. He was only four years old. I went back across on the rocks. I put little Joe on my shoulders. I got halfway and stepped on a rock and it gave way. Joe and I fell in the sewage over our heads. When I came back up, the children were screaming. Joe was being washed out into the Delaware River. I turned to see his little head bobbing up and down. I knew if he were going to be saved I was going to have to do it. I started swimming after him. I caught him by his sweater and pulled him up the bank. The children were screaming so loud the men from the sewage plant ran down to where we were. Some of the children ran screaming to our parents. Everyone came running down to the plant. Can you imagine the sight little Joe and I created? My hair was matted to my head from the raw waste. My shoes and coat and dress were ruined. Little Joe was just as bad. No one wanted to touch us but our parents. We were stinking real bad, and we began to vomit all over. Little Joe's Mom and my Mom sent home for sheets. They stripped us naked and wrapped us in sheets and left every piece of our Easter finery at the plant.

My Papa and Joe's Papa put some large rocks in place and went across and brought the other children back. They were too frightened to try it. They asked what had happened and why were we there. Fish, Bob, and Jack told them we were looking for violets, and they told how little Joe was being washed out into the Delaware River and how I swam out and brought him back. This was the first time I knew I had swum out and saved him because I never swam before. Mama and Papa nearly passed out because they knew I couldn't swim.

I could not stop crying and vomiting. Mama took me in back of the house and turned the hose on me. She tried washing my hair. It didn't do much good. I think she bathed me ten times with the hose before she took me in the house and washed me over and over in the tub with soap. She even put baking soda in the water. I still was stinking. She finally put some clothes on my weakened body. I was weak from all those baths and vomiting.

It was time for our Easter dinner. Everyone was at the table when I went in to sit down. They were all dressed. Mama had the proverbial ham, potato salad, collard greens, and candied yams. As I sat down my brother said, "Mama, I didn't know you cooked chittlins" (they stink!) My sisters laughed. Then one of them said, "Here's itty poo!" I jumped up and ran to my room feeling very hurt because my Papa and Mama laughed at me.

I again experienced the feeling of rejection. My ugly complex came back. They all came into the room and said they were just teasing me, but it was too late. I had gone back into my persecution complex. I couldn't stop crying. I cried myself to sleep in Mama's arms.

I was a little reluctant to return to school after our spring break. My friend Fish told everyone what had happened to me, but my teacher who was very wise and also my friend had everything under control, so my first day back wasn't too bad. I could still smell the odor in my hair, but it might have been my imagination. The day passed without any bad incidents. My teacher gave me a bottle of shampoo after school and told me to tell Mama to wash my hair in it. Mama washed my hair in it. I also took a bath in it. I was smelling so much better. It was twelve days since that day at the sewage plant.

Breaking up That Old Team of Mine

The summer came with all its beauty. We loved the summer because it seemed to bring the family closer with picnics and softball games. But nature was bound to intervene in more than one way. Lucy had already left the house to work in Philadelphia, but returned on most weekends, especially in the summer. But we were to lose another of the clan. My sister Nina was dreamy-eyed and somewhat absent-minded, but it was not the leisurely weather—Nina had a boyfriend. Dave was the center of Nina's world; the beautiful summer was the environment for a growing love between them.

Papa's strict rules about being home on time and his dramatic gun-cleaning before my sisters' beaus were losing their effect. One day Dave and Nina asked to speak to Mama and Papa *alone*. Vi and Nell and I were sent across the street to our cousins. Charles and Odell went off on their own but returned to eavesdrop at the side window of our home. The weather was warm and the window was open, so they heard everything.

Dave was a little clumsy in asking Papa's blessing on his request to marry Nina. He professed to love her, and Nina said she loved Dave very much. Charles and Odell were giggling and almost gave themselve away.

Lucy brought her handsome boyfriend to the house for Nina's

wedding, and people were all making plans, plans, plans. I was only eleven years old, but I caught on that the family would steadily grow smaller.

Nina and her husband Dave moved a short distance away, but their place was on my way to school. In a few years Nina had two babies, both delivered at home with the help of a midwife. I loved to push them in their coach.

So, we had lost one of our softball players and were soon to lose another. Lucy and Harry were to be married in August 1933 at home. Lucy was the most particular of the girls; everything had to be just so. She was fussy as a child—farming was not for her. She learned to be a hairdresser and then a seamstress and earned well at her job in Philadelphia.

Lucy made the dresses of her attendants, Nina and Odell—but would not let anyone see the wedding dress she made until the very day of the wedding. It was a beautiful white organza with ruffles and a pretty little veil. My cousins Fish and Bessy and I collected wildflowers to decorate the house, and Mama had all the curtains washed, starched, and ironed. The house was just right for the wedding.

Papa gave his second daughter away—to Harry, a handsome, grey-eyed man who promised to love my sister until the end of time. And so he did—they had five children, all girls. Odell played the piano and I sang two songs, "It's Only a Shanty in Old Shantytown" and "If You Don't Like My Apples, Don't Shake My Tree," an old blues song.

And so, the second of our teammates was married, but Lucy and Harry rented a home in East Riverton, New Jersey, near enough to attend our softball games. Lucy continued to play and Nina and Dave would drive over to cheer us on.

The Chicken Parade

It was a difficult summer however, with much unemployment. Papa was doing odd jobs to support us. Most of the families we knew were in the same situation as we were.

One of our Italian neighbors came over one night and asked my parents if they wanted to earn some money by taking the whole family to pick peas on the farm. Papa accepted, and the next day we walked to the farm and picked peas at twelve cents a basket. We worked on the farm picking string beans, tomatoes, peaches, and lima beans. In the fall we picked apples. We did quite well. My older sisters and brother did not like to work on the farm, but I sure did. I wanted to help Mama and Papa pay bills.

Early in the fall, Papa got a telegram saying his sister was dying in Norfolk, Virginia. We were very sad. Papa and Mama prepared to go to Virginia and stay a few days. They bought some groceries and paid the bills and gave my brother money to take care of us if they had to stay longer. As it turned out, they ended up staying three weeks longer, attending the funeral after my aunt died. By then, the food was running out. We were hungry. We asked Charles to get us some food, but he didn't have any money. He had been playing a card game called Pitty Pat with some of the other boys, and he had lost all of the food money.

Charles and Odell began whispering together. When those two put their heads together I was sure something was up. Odell was five years younger than Charles and smaller, but she could whip the living daylights out of him. They were so mischievous. They were always taking advantage of my naïveté, but they would have protected me to the death. Lucy wasn't at home; she had taken a job in Philadelphia. She was determined not to work on the farm at all. She said she would starve first.

Odell and Charles went outside, they were giggling. Odell told me to open the shed door and not close it until she said so. I tried to argue, but she looked at me hard and I did what I was told. She and Charles had a way of intimidating me. I went and sat by the open screen door. Odell put on two big pots of water to boil. I didn't know what they were going to do. I just sat there and waited.

Then, at about 5 PM, I heard the family whistle outside, and Odell whistled inside. Then I saw one of the funniest sights I have ever seen. Charles was walking slowly, coming around the corner of the house, and there was the strangest parade of chickens following him. He was dropping one kernel of corn at a time. He stepped over my legs, dropping corn, and those dumb chickens jumped over my legs as well. I was too mesmerized to move. Odell was at the opened front door. Charles kept right on through the house out the back door, and so did the chickens—all but two. Odell closed the door on the last two. She called me to close the back door. Charles threw the rest of the corn in the field and the other chickens went after it. He and Odell laughed until they cried. I was sitting on the floor looking at these two dumb chickens. They had taken over the kitchen.

Charles got a burlap bag, and he and Odell threw some corn in it and the chickens waddled inside. Charles went down to the swamp in back of our house and killed the chickens. Odell followed him with one pot of boiling water and then came back for the other pot. When they returned from the swamp, they had two of the cleanest chickens I had ever seen. Odell cut them up quickly, seasoned them, and put them on the stove to cook. They smelled wonderful. Odell put some vanilla and cinnamon in another pan to boil. She was trying to kill the smell of the cooking chicken. Charles had stolen those chickens from the man that lived up the street.

It began to smell like Thanksgiving. After the chickens had been cooking for about an hour, Charles asked Odell if she knew how to make dumplings. She said, "No," and Charles said he couldn't either.

Odell turned to me, "Mog, you always watch Mama cook. You can make dumplings. All you need is flour, baking powder, and lard. You go on and mix them, cook them for a half hour, then thicken it with flour." Well, they went outside and left me to make dumplings.

Mama had a new box of Clabber Girl baking powder. I mixed all the ingredients. I kept adding baking powder until I had used the entire box. I put the cut dumplings in the two pots and went outside. About a half hour later, I went inside to see about my dumplings, and to my amazement, there were dumplings all over the floor! They were climbing out of the pots like they were alive. I was so scared. The dumplings were riding out the kitchen door on a bed of foam.

I became hysterical. I began to scream, and I couldn't stop. Odell and Charles ran inside. Charles stepped on a dumpling, slid and fell down into a pile of them. Odell turned the stove off and went outside laughing. I looked over at Charles sitting in a pile of dumplings and started laughing myself. The dumplings were still moving on the floor!

Finally, Odell ran inside and told Charles that Mr. Kuzik was coming toward our house calling for his chickens. Odell went back outside. Mr. Kuzik asked if she had seen two of his chickens. Odell said, "No." Poor Mr. Kuzik never found out what had happened to his birds.

We cleaned up the mess. Charles got a fork and stuck it in the chickens; they still weren't done. They had been cooking for two hours and still weren't done. Baby Vi and Nell came home and we ate corn flakes for supper, then went to bed.

Charles and Odell cooked that chicken for two days. They

never got tender, but we ate them anyway. It turned out that they had stolen two old roosters, and those babies were tough! I had nightmares about dumplings, all kinds of dumplings, for two or three nights.

Maxie's Stage Show

I went to the American Store one day and overheard the manager talking to someone about needing a person to clean up after closing. I told him my Papa could do the job, and he told me to go and get him. I ran all the way home and took Papa there. Papa not only got the job, but he was given excess food and groceries for a while. I would walk down by the store occasionally to see where Papa worked but would not disturb him.

On one occasion, a few weeks later, some trucks came parading through the town with banners advertising Maxie's Stage Show. There were a lot of pretty women and men. The women were dancing as the orchestra played. We children ran behind the wagon and went to the field where they were setting up camp. It was fascinating. They gave us flyers to give out. It said they were having an amateur contest on Saturday. The prize would be twenty-five dollars. "Wow! Don't I wish I could win that money for Mama and Papa," I thought.

The next day, Fish and I went to see Miss Charlotte. She was a beautiful colored lady that was married to a rich German man. She had the prettiest clothes. She used to be a stage star. I told her I would like to enter the contest. I could sing pretty good, but I couldn't dance. She told me to come back every day and she would teach me the Charleston. She took one of her dresses—a beautiful blue. It was pleated all over. She cut it down and made me the prettiest dress you would want to see. She even made me bloomers out of the material that was left over from the dress. She put lace on them. The outfit was really pretty. She did my hair that Saturday and bought me new shoes and anklets. Miss Charlotte told Mama and Papa she was going to take me to the stage show and bring me home at ten o'clock. We went to her house and she dressed me in my beautiful dress, fixed my hair and put a ribbon in it, and she made me practice my song and dance as she played the piano for me. She was well satisfied at my performance, but I was getting nervous.

We arrived at the stage. The place was already packed. We went backstage. There were only three of us to perform; two men in their twenties, and there I was, about eleven years old. Well, those two men danced! They were good. Miss Charlotte took the piano stool and began to go up and down the scale to put me at ease. I walked out on stage and the people went wild, and that encouraged me. I opened my mouth and I began to sing, "It's Only a Shanty in Old Shantytown." I jazzed it up, and the crowd screamed. Then I went into my tap dance and buck dance, and I did the Charleston. Boy, I was really into it! I jumped up in the air and came down and did a split. I spun around and when I turned to the front, I was looking right in the face of Papa and Mama. I was so scared; I didn't know what to do. I turned around to get off that stage so fast the rubber in the waist of my bloomers broke. I ran over to Miss Charlotte.

When the man called us back for the applause, I refused to go. I won first prize. It was twenty-five dollars, and a lot of people kept putting money in my hands. Miss Charlotte took my free hand and took me over to Mama and Papa. People were still patting me on the head and giving me money. Mama and Papa weren't too mad. They told Miss Charlotte she should have told them that I was to perform. I didn't realize that they didn't know I was a contestant. Mr. Maxie, the owner of the show, was on the loud speaker saying, "Folks, come back every night! We are going to have little Maggie here every night!" Papa said, "NO!!! H—- NO!! NO!!" I gave Mama and Papa the money. When they counted it, it added up to over fifty dollars! That was a lot of money.

You know, God always took good care of me: One of the men in the show, Mr. Ernest, came to our house and told Mama and Papa that Mr. Maxie had a plan to take me with them when they moved and that they usually moved in the middle of the night. Mr. Ernest was very nice. I stayed with my aunt who helped Mama and Papa when they came from the South. Auntie had a big German shepherd, J.B., a great watchdog and my good friend. Papa and Charles kept the gun ready at all times, but nothing ever happened. Mr. Ernest remained after the show left, and married one of the girls from the next town.

The Vaccination

School days were the happiest time for me. I had more white girlfriends than black. We were always in each other's homes. Our movie houses were still segregated, but we always enjoyed going to the movies.

One day at school the doctor came in to see if the children had been properly vaccinated. They found out that all my sisters in school had never been vaccinated. They gave my parents ten days to have us vaccinated, or we would not be allowed to attend school. It broke my heart to think I could not go to school. My other sisters hated school, so they didn't care if they never went back.

Mama had them vaccinated, and they went back. Two days later, I was vaccinated, and became deathly ill. I became unconscious. I could vaguely remember doctors, Mama and Papa, aunts and cousins gathering around. I could hear them crying and praying. I could feel myself being lifted out of bed and gently put into a tub of ice water to bring down my high fever. They couldn't break it. Sister Willie Ann, Cousin Mamie, and Mama peeled whole white potatoes and packed my body with ice-cold slices. In no time the potatoes turned black. The doctor came back twice a day. He said the crisis was coming. I was going to die.

I was talking out of my head. I kept asking for Miss Jamison, the lady who had taught me the Bible. I kept calling her name. Sometime during my illness, Miss Jamison came, and she asked everyone to go downstairs and rest. Miss Jamison wrapped me in a sheet and anointed me with oil. She held me and began talking what sounded like gibberish. Later, I realized she was praying in tongues to the Lord, interceding for my life. She rocked me back and forth.

It was as if something had been holding my body in a grip; it finally let go. The fever had broken. For the first time in ten days I fell into a natural sleep. Mama led everyone back upstairs. They didn't quite trust Miss Jamison. Miss Jamison had the Holy Ghost, and at that time, the Baptist people didn't understand about the Holy Ghost. Miss Jamison told Mama that I had smallpox, which was unheard of at that time. The doctor said I was the only case in over fifty years. They all cried and thanked God and Miss Jamison. Everyone treated Miss Jamison better after that. I heard Mama say she was told sometime ago that a lot of things were going to happen to Mog, "I really thought she would die this time, but thank God she's alive."

Softball and Boys

I was getting ready to graduate and go on to high school. There were only four of us graduating in our all-black school. We had to have our graduation with the white eighth grade. Our teacher had taught us not to hang back, to participate whenever we could. She made me try for valedictorian, but I lost out. At the auditorium I did the lawyer's speech from "The Merchant of Venice," the one that starts with "The quality of Mercy is not strained. It droppeth as the gentle rain from Heaven." The four black graduates had planned to sing "Danny Boy," and we rehearsed it diligently until our soul harmony was perfect. We were hurt to learn that we would not be allowed to sing it. Instead the entire graduating class would sing "Danny Boy." We were so disappointed that at graduation, we refused to open our mouths when they sang "Danny Boy." Perhaps it was strange to some to hear black children singing "Danny Boy," but we had the talent.

I found high school very challenging. My cousin Fish and I did our best to make the honor roll. We excelled in sports at school. There was one thorn in our side in high school; there was one teacher that gave blacks a hard time. I overheard this teacher say to another that he didn't like teaching Negroes because they had inferior brains. He said we were insignificant, inhuman insects. I told my parents and they went to the principal, but nothing was done. That teacher remained unfriendly and inconsiderate of blacks.

After six months in high school, my parents announced we had rented a large home in another town. I was heartbroken. I didn't want to leave Riverside. Mama and Papa said I could stay with Nina and her family for the remainder of the school year. My family moved two towns over from Riverside, to Beverly, New Jersey. It was a small town. I would go there on the weekends. Nina and her husband had a very handsome roomer staying at their house. He was a friend of her husband, a man named John Morris. My parents thought a lot of him.

After the school year was over, I had to leave my best friend and cousin Fish and all my schoolmates in Riverside. But, I found that it was nice being in a new town. Now that I was a teenager, I had slimmed down and lost my baby fat. I began to fill out here and there. Boys started walking by my house a lot. My sister Nell had a boyfriend. At night, we would sit on our porch with several local boys. Papa would come outside and clean his gun in front of everyone. He intimidated the boys, and they were really afraid of him.

One evening all the sisters got together to play the boys in softball. We beat them so badly that they wandered home in dejection. We were so enthusiastic about our talent that we formed a softball team. It was the beginning of a long, successful career in amateur softball. We joined a league and set quite a few records. Eventually we were sponsored by different companies. I was the pitcher, Odell played first base, Lucy center field, Vi at shortstop, Nell was at third base. We had made friends with a family named Andrews who lived in South Beverly. Marion, Dorothy, and Jane Andrews played softball, so they joined our team. Our team was unbeatable for years, and so was our friendship with the Andrews sisters, who are close to us today. We played from Chester, Pennsylvania, through Burlington County, New Jersey, all the way east and north to New York. We became well-known over a very large area. A scout asked my parents if I could go to California and play for the Americanettes. It broke my heart when they said, "No." But I wasn't out of school yet, and my parents knew best.

We lived one block from the Delaware River, where there was a well-kept field along the bank. A rich man in town gave the hitters one dollar for home runs, and five dollars for putting the ball in the river, and if I pitched a shutout he gave me ten! We made a lot of money. People would come from all over to see us play. Our uniforms were navy blue satin shorts, with white and blue blouses, white sneakers, and blue socks. We were sponsored by Keeler's meat market. Our names were stitched on the back of our blouses. We really loved strutting our stuff. Papa and the whole family traveled with us, even up to New York. Nina's roomer, John Morris, went along as well. He never missed a game.

The city put a recreation building down by the Delaware River. When we finished a game, we would go down there and dance. Sometimes several families would come down and stay all night if the weather were hot. They would spread out blankets and put their children down to sleep. Our boyfriends would join us down by the river.

Boys that we had met out of town started coming to see us play. They would come to our house, and we would sit outside beneath the porch light. Inevitably, Papa would come out and clean his gun. He had the cleanest gun in town! Whenever we showed interest in a boy, Papa would display his gun and they wouldn't come around anymore. I'm surprised the last four girls ever got married. Papa would have been satisfied if we had all become nuns!

We devised a plan to beat Papa at his own game. If we really liked a fellow, we would laugh and make fun of him, and tell Papa to be sure and come out to clean his gun. Papa would assume that the boy was not a threat and would stay inside. We really put one over on him , because in later years, Vi and Nell kept company and married their guys, two brothers who Papa never bothered to scare away.

Odell, Nell, and I traveled together a lot. Odell met a very nice young man from Maryland, and they were going steady, well as steady as Papa would let them! There was always a string of girls coming around using us sisters to get to Charles. I couldn't blame them, for my brother was very handsome, and he knew it and used that fact until the day he died. The women ruined him, always showering him with gifts and money. He could have a date seven nights a week, but Papa and Mama put their feet down on such behavior; it soon caused a problem, and Charles moved out.

In school, groups of girls would get together and talk about sex. I didn't have any input because I was ignorant about sex. Mama had never talked to me about it, she was too embarrassed. When I was fourteen and became a young lady, I was petrified at what was happening. My teacher at that time came to my rescue and told me about the changes taking place in my body. By the time I turned fifteen, my hormones were jumping. I found the transition into womanhood a very confusing process. I would be very happy at times, then my mood would turn pensive. With the guidance of my black teacher, I made it through an awkward adolescence. Those girls at school told some of the craziest stories about sex. I vowed that when I got married and had children, I was going to set them straight about the facts of life.

Learning A Trade

Our holidays during my high school years were rather nice. They weren't as sumptuous up North as they had been at home down South, but my Papa and Mama kept us clothed and fed. They still had that deep southern pride about them. One Thanksgiving Eve, a lady came and told Mama she was having a Thanksgiving dinner for twenty people, and she needed someone to cook and serve. She had heard about Mama being a good southern cook and wanted her to cook for her. Mama had to refuse.

I followed the lady outside. I told her I could and would do it. She looked at me and said she didn't think I could do it. I assured her I could. I was five feet seven inches, and weighed one-hundred twenty-nine pounds. She gave me her address and told me to come that afternoon and look things over.

I didn't tell Mama and Papa what I was going to do. I asked

Mama how to cook certain foods. I had learned a lot at this age about cooking. In the afternoon that Thanksgiving Eve, I went tothe lady's home. She showed me all kinds of foods: turkey, corn bread stuffing, squash, string beans, collard greens, and more. I knew it wouldn't be a problem. I prepared the things I could, then I went home.

I told Mama I was invited out to Thanksgiving dinner. I asked her permission because she wanted everyone at the table at meal-times, especially on holidays. The lady wanted sweet potato biscuits. I had never made any, but I had seen Mama make them. I sure did some praying before and during the cooking of that Thanksgiving feast for twenty people. It was a great success. She gave me twenty-five dollars, which was to me, a fortune. Some of her guests thanked me and also tipped me.

After that dinner, I was called on for holidays and fancy parties. I really learned a lot. They never knew that I was new at it. Everywhere I went, I kept my eyes opened so I could learn all that was possible to learn. I was called on by the rich people to decorate for weddings, showers, and regular parties. I sure used my imagination. I bought every book about the movie stars and pictures of their homes. I went to the movies a lot—it only cost ten cents. I always carried a pen and paper with me to jot down pertinent facts I could use in deco-rating, flower arranging, table setting, and food preparation. That's how I learned a lot about entertaining. I told my Mama after that Thanksgiving about my cooking the dinner for twenty. I gave Mama twenty dollars and I kept five plus the tips.

I prepared a number of meals for this woman who remained my friend for a number of years. I was not quite seventeen at the time. I received many beautiful clothes from that nice lady.

John Morris

At every family gathering my sister's roomer, John Morris, was there. He was like one of the family. Whenever Mama let Odell, Nell, and me attend dances, John came along. Whenever we went to par-ties, he was always parked somewhere near. He was older than we were, and very protective. He had never married. He told my parents that he was waiting to find that special girl. He said his mother had prayed to God to send him the right wife. He was one of the nicest people I had ever met.

I was very glad about his presence one night. I loved to dance and I won several prizes for dancing. I had a girlfriend from Newark and she taught me all of the newest dances before they got to South Jersey. This night, I went to a dance with some girls. Mama would never let me go alone. During the dance, the girls left with some boys without telling me. They told another fellow to take me home. He came up to me after the dance and said, "The girls left. Can I take you home." I didn't have any other way to get home, so I agreed.

We started toward home, and I bent down and took my high-heeled shoes off. When I looked up, he had turned the car into some woods. When we stopped, he developed more arms than an octopus, and his hands were pawing me all over. I took my shoe and hit him over the head. I dropped the shoe and started blowing the horn. He opened the car door and dragged me outside. We were wrestling all over the ground. I was using everything Papa and Charles taught me to defend myself. I was tall and thin, a real wildcat, and I was giving him a rough time. He grabbed me again, but as he stood over me he was suddenly lifted off the ground and slammed down hard. Someone was slapping him around. I didn't know who it was, so I grabbed a big tree limb and climbed in the car and locked the doors. I was ragged and breathless and began to pray.

The man who came to my rescue started toward the car. I began to blow the horn and scream, brandishing the tree limb. As he moved into the car's headlights, I was relieved to see it was John Morris. Somehow when John appeared, I felt strongly that God had been taking care of me. Before John Morris took me home, he told that fellow if he or anyone ever harmed me, they would have to answer to him. Mama and Papa were very upset, but John calmed them down. With John looking after me, they knew I was in good hands.

The Right Man

Odell and her boyfriend had fallen in love and were planning to get married. We decorated the house for their wedding and Mama, Nina, and Lucy did a lot of cooking. I helped Odell pick out a dress. She was married at home, then she and her husband got a room in town. I missed her very much.

With my last year of high school ahead, I realized I was the oldest one living at home. I had a boyfriend who used to walk me to the train to go to school. One day he came to see me and told me he loved me. He put a ring on my finger and asked me to elope. The girls in school were always boasting about their boyfriends. Some of them sported rings and said they were going to quit school and get married. I think I agreed to elope just to prove something to them, to prove something to myself.

I told Odell about our plans. My friend borrowed a car. The idea was to drive to Philadelphia to pick up another couple, who were going to elope with us, and continue on to Elkton, Maryland. In the meantime, Odell had told Mama and Papa what we were up to. They contacted his parents, and everyone piled in their cars to head us off.

Once we had gotten on the road, I realized it was a mistake. I didn't know what I was doing, I was getting cold feet. I was trying to think of ways to get out of it. My problems were solved when we crossed into Pennsylvania. There were my family and John Morris, my friend's father and mother, and a policeman. We stopped the car and Papa took my hand and put me in John's car. Charles told my friend never to see me again or he would kill him. "If he doesn't," John said, "I will!" I didn't cry or carry on like my family expected me to do. I was praising the Lord on the way home.

One night I got out of bed to go to the bathroom and heard Mama and Papa praying. They were asking the Lord for guidance. Mama said, "Lord, Mog needs a husband that will love and cherish her. Lord, let her see this wonderful man you have sent her already. She is so tender-hearted and kind. We thank you for sending her the right man. Please open her eyes so she will recognize whom you have sent her."

You can imagine how shocked I was. I didn't have the slightest idea whom they were talking about. I shook my head in bewilderment and went to sleep, never telling them what I had overheard.

On weekends my sisters, their husbands and children gathered at home. One Saturday Nina's husband, Dave, said, "Mog, school is almost out and you'll graduate. What are you going to do?"

"I am going to North Carolina and continue my education," I replied.

During the evening, John asked Mama if he could take me to a movie. Everyone was grinning when we left. It was a very romantic movie, and I cried. I noticed how tenderly John held my hand.

On the way home, we parked down at the river. I was becoming uneasy because John seemed distracted, there was something on his mind. Then this beautiful man turned to me and said, "Please

73

don't go to North Carolina. I'm in love with you, and I want to marry you."

I was stunned. He began telling me how he had waited since I was fifteen years old for me to grow up. My entire family knew how he felt. They understood when I went to parties and dances that John would be there to protect me.

He said, "I became afraid when you began to date other fellows, especially when you were going to elope. I started to tell you then, but I wanted you to grow up first." As we sat in his car by the river, John quietly poured out his heart to me. He said he had girlfriends before, but he hadn't met anyone that he wanted to marry. I looked at this handsome man and I wondered why he wanted me. He was six foot three, a handsome guy who was a mixture of black, English, Indian, and Puerto Rican. By far the most handsome man I had ever seen. I wasn't beautiful like my sisters and girlfriends, and I asked him why. He told me I was beautiful and that my gentleness and kind spirit showed in my face. I was glad that John had not let his feelings be known before because I wasn't mature enough at that time. I was becoming self-conscious with John. As I looked at him bashfully, something stirred in my heart, something so tender I began to cry. I was so darn confused. He took me in his big arms until I stopped crying. He told me to take my time to make up my mind. My hormones were jumping all over the place, I had such strong feelings for John.

At home I realized everyone knew John was going to propose. I excused myself and went to bed. I couldn't sleep. All night his handsome face monopolized my mind. I had about thirty-five more days before I would finish high school, and I could do nothing but think of John. I told Mama I wanted to talk to her after school. She said God had answered her prayers, but the final decision had to be mine. She only wanted me to be happy. I couldn't open up and tell Mama how I felt.

I turned to my former school teacher for some guidance. I could always talk to her. She talked frankly, and told me a lot of things I needed to know. She was hoping I would go to college. I told her finances were bad, and I couldn't go. She said if and when I got married, to never stop learning; to continue my reading, my poetry and short story writing. I felt very good after I left her.

Mama told John he could take me out only on Saturdays, and the rest of the time visit me at home. John courted me nicely. I was going to be nineteen in about a year and a half. He said we would wait until I was nineteen. Nell and Vi were going with two brothers and Nell was getting serious.

One evening Nell and her boyfriend, Eugene, came home and announced they wanted to get married. Papa and Mama talked to them, and decided they would have to wait until Nell was seventeen. Nell was seventeen and Eugene was nineteen when they were married. A lot of people said it wouldn't last long. Eugene and Nell were married fifty-two years when he died.

After I had finished school one day, John took me out to dinner. He gave me a dozen yellow roses. Afterward, we drove to my favorite spot, near the river in front of my house. We walked along the river bank holding hands. He turned to me in the moonlight, took me in his arms and kissed me. He had kissed me before, but it never affected me like this! I knew then that I was in love with him. There on the river bank, John asked me again to become his wife. I said yes. He placed a beautiful ring on my finger and he put his two hands around my waist and lifted me up in the air.

The following Sunday, John took me to his parent's home for dinner. I knew them quite well for we attended the same church. I was very active in church work, heading youth programs and writing children's programs for Easter Days and Christmas. John's parents were beautiful people. His mother was a very tall, stately woman with her hair done up in a large bun. She looked like a real Indian with high cheekbones, copper-colored skin and black, velvety eyes. When she let her hair down, it fell to the back of her thighs. John's father was often mistaken for white. He was part English and part Puerto Rican, with a very fair complexion, auburn hair and greenish-blue eyes. I could see where John got his good looks. His parents received me with open arms and his Mom said, "John, this is the only one I would accept as my daughter because I know her to be a Christian girl. I have seen her work in church ever since she was very young." We began planning.

Mama and Papa told me they could give me a small, home wedding. I went to work part-time in a home to make money and also worked on the farm. John didn't like the fact that I was working. He told me I could have a large wedding—as big as I wanted—he would pay for it. He also told me we could travel anywhere in the world. It was well-known that John was one of the richest colored men around. At our reception, one of my friends told me people were saying I married John for his money. I told her I never asked him what he had. I wasn't interested in his bank account. I was angry that anyone would think so little of me. I asked Mama and Papa about it. They said they never asked him anything as personal as that. I told John I didn't want him paying for my wedding, and he respected my wishes.

On June the 27th, 1940, at the age of nineteen, I became the wife of John Morris. Nina was my matron of honor, one of my girl friends was my bridesmaid. We were married in John's parent's house, and later had a reception at my folks.

My dress was white, very tight in the waist and flared out in the princess style, high-necked, with three quarter sleeves and white satin scallops around the sleeve edges and the neckline. The dress was a form-fitting size six. I had white pumps and a little hat with flowers with a little veil on it, white gloves, and a purse. The entire outfit cost less than seventy dollars.

We both cried when we were married. John promised to cherish and love me, protect me, and provide for me. Through four children and forty-one years, he kept his word. I was always treated like a queen, even after my size six dress and twenty-four inch waist disappeared.

John's mother fixed us two private rooms on the second floor. Several of his relatives from Maryland and North Carolina arrived the day after the wedding. They sent my mother-in-law upstairs to get me, but I was too embarrassed to come down. John went down and talked to them. I thought they would tease me. That afternoon at dinner I met them all. They teased John about robbing the cradle and said they were delighted to have me in the family. I chose to go to New York for one week of our honeymoon and to spend one week in Atlantic City. John and I left for New York in a brand new Ford.

Honeymoon

I had been to New York several times before, but I didn't spend any time sightseeing because we were there to play ball. John had made reservations at the Theresa Hotel. We met Joe Louis the boxer and his manager on the elevator one morning. We met Lena Horne and Count Basie at the hotel. John took it all in stride, but I was very excited and thrilled, and John made me feel very special. We all had dinner at the same time at the hotel. We went sightseeing. We went to shows and the movies. John said, "Anything—and I mean anything— you want, regardless of cost, you can have it!" I wanted everything I saw, but being very careful of spending money all my life, I chose very little. We had a beautiful, romantic horse-and-buggy ride with another couple we met. It was really heaven on earth there in New York— seven wonderful days in New York City.

We traveled to Atlantic City for another week of our honeymoon. Oh, it was so beautiful. We stayed in a beautiful tourist home. We had the bridal suite. The proprietor had the room decked out with flowers. There was a lovely fragrance throughout the room. There was a bottle of champagne cooling in a container. The covers on the bed were turned back and a gift for me, the bride, was an exquisite pink peignoir set. Oh! It was beautiful. Our room had a large sliding door that enabled us to look at the ocean. It had a private parking place for our car. Oh, no movie star ever had it so beautiful. In one corner of the room was a little ice cream table and two chairs. The table was covered with a damask cloth. There was a pink candle in a crystal holder and a vase filled with fresh flowers.

We bathed and decided we would stay in that afternoon and rest. We were really exhausted. The trip from New York was a long one. We put on our lounge wear and ordered our dinner served in our room. The proprietor came and put our table in front of the opened doors and set it. I will never forget that day or any of the days of a perfect two-week honeymoon with the most handsome, gentle, loving man in my life. Anything I wanted I had only to ask. I asked for very little, and what I didn't ask for he purchased anyhow. We did a lot of sightseeing in the town, and also lay on the beach on blankets. God made us some very special weather. The dinner at our suite was most delightful. There was fresh broiled trout, a special garden salad, and fresh corn on the cob. For dessert we had homemade lemon cake with lemon sauce and lemonade. It was delicious.

While we were on the beach one afternoon, I was approached by a woman and man. He asked if I were John's wife. I said, "Yes." They asked me to stand up, and John being very protective of me asked why. They said they were scouts for the "Miss Fine Brown Frame" contest. We said, "What does that have to do with us?" They said they were scouting Atlantic City beaches this week. They had found ten girls to compete. I stood up and the lady said, "Perfect!" She put her hands on my waist and John said, "That's enough! Get your hands off my wife!" They apologized and explained everything, and then the woman took out a pad from her purse. The man had a measuring tape. They asked John if they could take my measurements. He said, "It's up to my wife." I said, "Let the lady take it" and she said, "G— D—-!" "Look at this!" He looked at it and said, "Perfect!" They had written something down and they said, "Look." We looked and the measurements said, "36, 24, 36!" I was five feet, seven inches tall.

They asked me if I would like to be in the contest that would be held on the boardwalk one month from the date. I told them I didn't have the looks to be in it. I told them they would have pretty girls in it. They said my face and figure could really give the other contestants a good run for the money. They asked me if I had any talent. I said I could sing for my own amusement and could dance a little. They asked us to come to the talent tryouts that night. I sang "I'll Get Along Somehow." I had heard Lena Horne sing it. I did very well in the contest for singing. It was very exciting.

I could see John didn't like my strutting around in a bathing suit, so I decided not to enter, but what I experienced taught me a lot. Anyway, I was on a very romantic honeymoon that was more important to me than any contest. I don't know whether or not I might have won. It was not important to me. I had a very handsome new husband and that was enough for me. After a lot of sightseeing and walking, hand in hand, around the town, we had to say goodbye to Atlantic City. It was a memorable visit

The place where we stayed on our honeymoon was torn down in later years to build a casino. Our ride home was heavenly. We took it very slowly, hating for our honeymoon to end. We arrived home late and went to bed. We went to church the next day for the first time as man and wife. It was delightful. John's Mom fixed us a nice dinner and some well-wishers came by and brought us some delightful presents. After they left, we went for a nice leisurely drive in the country. We came back and went by my parent's home. All of my crazy sisters were there, and they teased me until I cried from embarrassment. They asked me some awful questions and gave me some awful advice until Mama had to come and rescue me. Even Nell who is younger than I and who married six months before I did got in on the kidding. She said they did the same to her. My sisters were the craziest bunch you would want to see. I did not look forward to my first Saturday's visit as a married couple to my parent's home.

The next morning John went to work. I came down and ate breakfast and went upstairs and slept all day. I didn't have any work to do because my mother-in-law did everything. After two weeks, Mama came over and told Mrs. Morris I was to cook for my husband and I was to do our laundry and do half the housework. I was very glad because I didn't have anything to do but go out walking. I was never the kind to go out visiting all the time. It was a habit I never formed, perhaps because our family was big and very clannish. We were sufficient unto ourselves.

All in the Family

On Saturdays my sisters and their familys came to Mama's. We all prepared a lot of food, I mean a lot. The men went next door to play cards and pool, and all of the children went outside to play. I cooked the sweet potato pies, and early in the afternoon we ate. There were about twenty-three of us at that time, initiating John into this crazy family. It was hilarious. They teased us to death. We had never laughed so much.

My sisters and brother began to reminisce about the past. They had me in stitches. Charles began by telling about something funny that Vi did. On one occasion, our parents had gone to Virginia and had left him in charge of us as they usually did. Charles spent most of the money. One day Charles bought a loaf of bread and one can of pork and beans and that's all we had for supper. He divided the beans into four portions, which were small indeed. We sat down to eat, and Vi said, "I'll be there soon." Charles kept going to the stove and was eating out of the pan where the beans were. When I got up to feed Vi, there were only eight beans left. I gave them to Vi. She took four slices of bread and put one bean on one corner of each of two slices. She then put the tops on the two slices and cut each sandwich in half. She then cut each half in half, and when she got finished, she had eight quarter sandwiches with one bean in each sandwich, and she said, "I have more than you all. I have eight sandwiches!" From then on we called her "club sandwich!"

Well, Odell had an anecdote to tell John. Papa used to take us on the railroad to pick up coal. The conductor got used to Papa and his family, and they began to throw extra coal out for us and they also threw money out for us kids. Odell got tired picking up coal all the time, so one day she wrote a note and on it she told the conductor please throw a lot of coal out because she was tired of picking it up. She signed her name to it. The trainmen and firemen knew all of us by name. The next day the train slowed down and there were two men at the door and they threw out three burlap bags full of coal and a letter addressed to Odell. All we had to do was to have Papa and Charles pick up the bags and put them in the wagon. Odell's letter said, "Take a break for two days. We will be back in three days!" We all had to laugh at the boldness of Odell, but we were thankful for the coal because we were a little ashamed to go out there on the tracks, but Papa said we wouldn't be ashamed to sit by the stove and get warm. Of course John and everyone had a big laugh.

Odell said, "John, we've got something to tell you about the gal you married. We all had gone out to shop with Mama, but Mog stayed home, and when we got home, she had her boyfriend there and when he stood up we were quite surprised to see he had his pants on The wrong side and the pockets lining was on the outside. We all laughed, but Mama asked him why did he have them on like that. He told her he took them right off the line when they were drying, he was in such a hurry to come to see me he hadn't noticed anything but they were still damp. There was no problem with Mama believing Mog. We all sure teased Mog about it. We were glad Papa wasn't there. He would have gotten his gun and then asked questions!" Oh, that was the first of many Saturdays for John with my great big, crazy, wonderful family.

John told the family about our honeymoon adventures—not all of it of course! He told them about the contest for "Miss Fine Brown Frame" and about my refusal to enter it even though I was qualified. Mama and Papa said, "She knows better than to go prancing around in a bathing suit! Married or not, she would have been in trouble with us!"

We had some very good and happy days. Many a Saturday and Sunday was spent at my parent's home. There was always a lot of singing. Odell and her husband seemed to be having problems. We all were praying that they would resolve them because they truly loved one another.

I was working very much at church. At times I participated around the county on youth programs and other types of services. I loved doing dramatic readings and my favorite readings were from James Weldan's book, *God's Trombone*. I memorized the whole book. I tried to work in different auxiliaries in church right along with Mama and my mother-in-law. Our prayers were answered for Odell and her husband reconciled and we were happy because we all loved him.

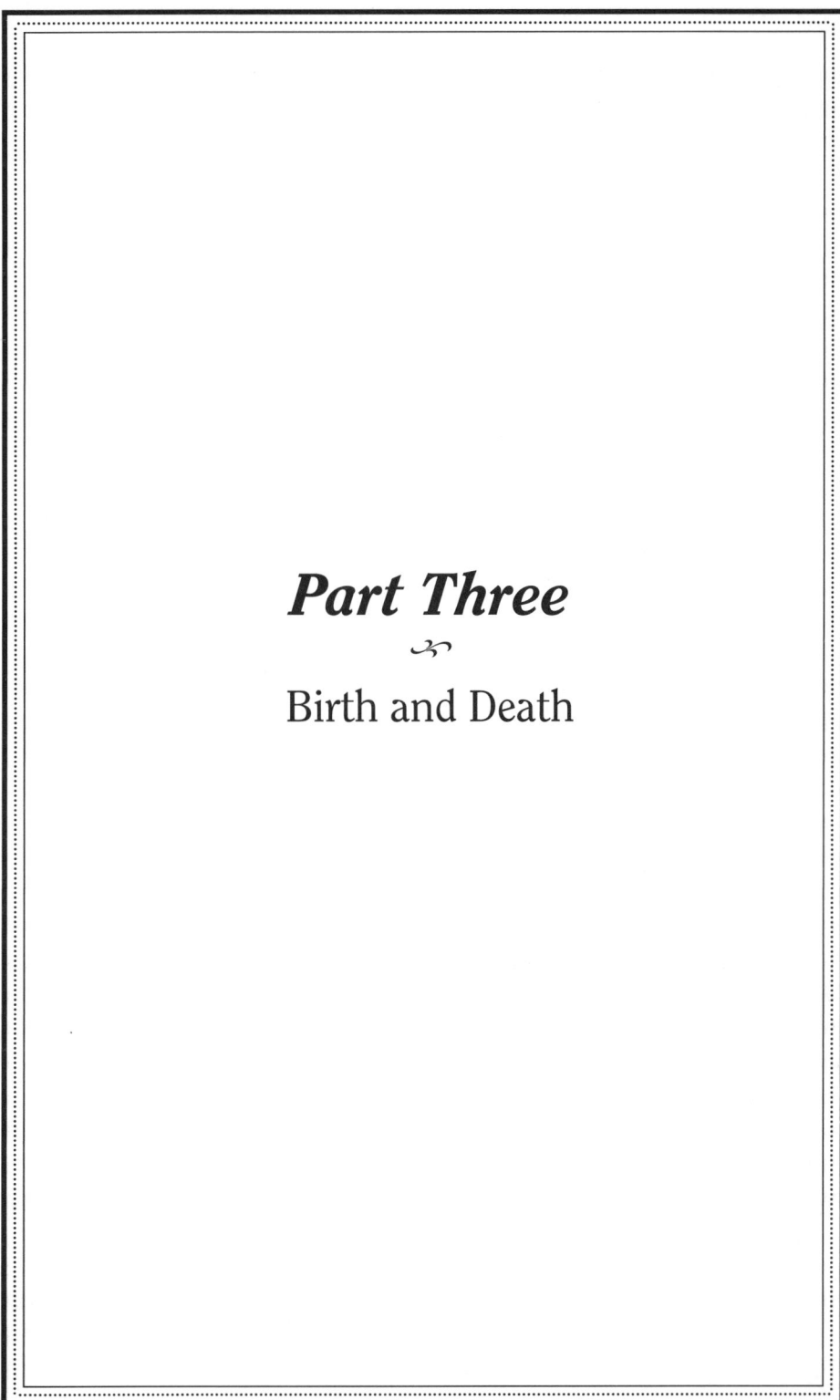

Part Three

Birth and Death

One Saturday in January we were at Mama's house cooking pork chops when Nell fainted. When she came to, she began to throw up. My sisters teased her that she was pregnant. She was so surprised. She looked like a little girl. Nina looked at me and said, "Mog, you're in the family way." Well, that really caught me off guard.

All of my childhood insecurities came back, my fears of being rejected. I thought Nina said I was in the family's way! I didn't understand the other meaning. Mama noticed the look on my face and followed me out of the room. "What's wrong Mog?" she asked. I told her I was confused. I didn't know I was in the family's way. I thought they all loved me. She laughed and called me a nut, then to my relief, explained what Nina meant.

Two months later it was my turn to faint and throw up. Then Lucy began to do the same. Mama and Papa had four grandchildren born in one year. Nell had a boy. Nina and Lucy had girls. On Christmas Eve, 1941, at 6:30 AM, I went into labor. On December 25th at 6:30 AM my Peggy Ann was born. The baby doll I had always wanted for Christmas was finally delivered. I had a beautiful girl. When I held her in my arms, I experienced an intense bonding with this little human being. I couldn't stop crying. I was in awe of this birth, and soon forgot all of the pain and discomfort. John was ecstatic.

After seeing most of her sisters give birth, Odell and her husband wanted a child, and she soon became pregnant. But in nine months Odell's baby was stillborn. She and her husband were heartbroken. To help her overcome this tragedy, we shared our babies with her. We had a wonderful time taking care of our children. A few weeks later, Odell's husband was inducted into the service, and he went off to basic training.

We had been noticing Mama wasn't as lively as she had been.

She was lying around a lot. My mother-in-law, in the meantime, had become very ill and was in the hospital. Weeks went by and neither of their conditions improved. I was losing two mothers, and the strain was overbearing. John's mother was growing worse by the day, and my Mama was in and out of a sickbed. She had lost her beautiful vibrancy.

Two months after being admitted to the hospital, my mother-in-law died. Our family grieved terribly. We took my mother-in-law to be buried in Maryland. We arrived home about one o'clock the next morning, and went over to Mama's.

In the house, everyone rushed toward me and told me to see Mama. She was slipping away, and the doctor had been coming every other day. I ran upstairs.

"I was waiting for you to come home," Mama said. "I know your mother-in-law died." I was surprised because no one had told her. We called the ambulance and they rushed her to a hospital in Philadelphia. Papa, Nina, and Charles went with her. We stayed up all night awaiting word. Around eleven o'clock the next morning, Papa, Nina, and Charles returned. We knew by the look on their faces that our beloved Mama had died. The woman I thought was indestructible, my friend and confidante, had died. It was hard to believe, but it was true.

Mama died seven days after my mother-in-law. It was awfully hard on all of us. We were always a very close-knit family. We became wild in our grief. In less than a half hour it seemed as if the entire town had come to pay their respects. The town grieved along with our family. It was one of the hardest weeks of my life. I saw both of my mothers buried within eight days. I thanked God for my husband John. Even though he was grieving for his mother, he took time to console us.

Mama's funeral was somewhat hazy. My emotions were in denial. Even as I sat looking at Mama in her casket, it all seemed so distant, like a bad dream. She had the most beautiful smile on her face. She was at peace. She had earned her place on earth, and God had rewarded her a place with Him. She had truly been a mother, the kind God would have all mothers to be. She had served her husband and children well. She would have gladly given up her life for anyone of us. We really missed her, but life must continue.

My father-in-law went to live with his daughter and her family. John and I were left to live in the fourteen-room family house. I didn't like living in such a large home. We were very glad we had our little girl to take care of. She kept me busy while John was at work. We did not live too far from Mrs. Jamison's, and the all-black school I attended when we moved from the South. I decided I was going to take my little girl to see Mrs. Jamison, for she had been a very important influence in my life.

Mrs. Jamison's hair was turning gray, and she wore her clothes long like a holy lady. She had a beautiful glow about her. I realized it was the presence of the the Holy Spirit. I told her I hoped that one day I would have that beautiful glow and she promised me I would. I told Mrs. Jamison all about myself, while she held my little girl very close. After visiting awhile, I invited her to our home. She said the town still treated her coldly, and they may not like her visiting. I told her I wasn't worried, our friendship was more important to me than what people thought.

Our family was changing rapidly with each year. My brother Charles moved to California, and after a few visits home, he passed away at the age of forty. My baby sister Vi had fallen in love with her boyfriend, and they were married. So, with Vi and Nell married to two brothers, all the sisters were married.

In Beverly, where my sisters were living, some beautiful brick town houses were being built. Each of my sisters and their husbands decided to apply for one. My father and his new wife also applied. Papa had married Miss Laura, the woman who once lived across the street from us when we were down South. She did not want too much to do with us, so we stopped meeting at Papa's home on Saturday nights. She didn't want us coming around to see Papa, so everyone congregated at our big home. At first, we cried a lot because we missed Mama. We invited our stepmother to join us. She came a few times, and we made her feel welcome, but she was aloof. She put a damper on our gatherings.

I used to work for the housing director and his wife, and when the new homes were finally finished, I asked him to let me be the first to move in, which I did—into a smaller, more manageable home. There were eight adjoining homes in two sections, and each section had four homes. My sisters moved in one by one, then Papa and his wife.

I had the first baby born in the new settlement, a boy, John R., Jr. He had auburn hair and greenish-blue eyes. Three of us sisters had children within three months of each other. We were very wrapped up in the children. John loved for me to take our son and daughter to meet him as he came out of work. The men would all stop and play with our children.

Yes, our family was changing and growing, but in many ways it was growing closer. We sisters would do our major cleaning on Friday. We would have our children and ourselves all cleaned and dressed by the time our husbands came home. So many times we found ourselves cooking the same meal without the other knowing what we were cooking beforehand! We would shop separately only to find we had bought our children nearly identical outfits and usually the same color. There wasn't any family as close as ours.

There is a funny example of our closeness. All the sisters, even the ones who lived out of town, loved the soap stories. One afternoon we all were in our respective homes cooking and looking at the "Edge of Night." Well, Mike Carr was the main character along with his wife, named Peggy. They were so in love with each other. Mike was driving up to his home. His wife ran to meet him. She was struck by a car. Mike jumped out of his car and ran to pick her up. She died in his arms. We all cried, coming out of our homes, looking for each other. Other women saw us and cried with us. John and the husbands of my sisters and neighbors came up. They asked, "What's wrong?" John took me in his arms. I said, "She's dead!" He said, "Who?" I said, "Peggy." He thought I meant our Peggy. He went to pieces. We looked and saw smoke coming out of the house and we realized our dinner had burned up. After we told our husbands who Peggy was, they hit the ceiling. That was the first time I had heard John curse. We sisters really laughed about it for a long time.

In the summer we would barbecue a whole pig, and we would have cookouts to end all cookouts. Friends and relatives would come from all over to visit. We sisters were still playing baseball. We would bundle our families in our respective cars and away we all traveled, far and wide. We played until we were pregnant, and after giving birth, we would start up again.

The Breakdown

Everything was going well and I felt my life was just about perfect. I had a handsome husband, two beautiful children, a pretty home. John had given me a brand-new car. Our son, whom we called Butch, was eleven months old and learning to walk. He held onto furniture and was delighted with each step. He had four teeth and was always grinning. He could say "DaDa," "Mama," "Pedeen" for Pegeen, his sister. We were proud of his small accomplishments.

One afternoon, John and I went shopping. We hired a fourteen-year-old girl whom we had used before to babysit. We gave the sitter instructions about the children. It was the week of Thanksgiving and rather cold. We had a coal stove, and we heated the house warmly and had banked the stove so it would keep warm. We liked to keep the temperature at sixty-eight degrees at all times. We had made snacks for them. We kissed our babies and went shopping. That was the last peaceful, worry-free moment we were to have in a long time.

John and I were away for two and a half hours. When we returned and parked in front of the house, I suddenly got an awful knot in my stomach. I became very apprehensive and bolted out of the car so fast that it startled John. In the cold weather the door knob was warm. Something was wrong. I flung open the door. Everything looked normal. My little girl was coloring in her book, but her rompers were off. The baby sitter was lying on the couch reading comic books with a stack of sandwiches on the table. It was so hot inside it took my breath away.

I looked at my baby, and my heart nearly stopped. The baby was sitting in his highchair. He was asleep with his head leaning against the wall. On the surface everything looked normal, but I had this feeling in my heart that something was wrong. I was drawn to my baby, and as I touched him, he slumped over. I took him in my arms and I realized he was unconscious. I began to scream. John came running in and asked, "What's wrong. Why is it so hot in here?" He took the baby. We tried to wake him, but nothing happened. We called the police and an ambulance. They gave him oxygen and mouth-to-mouth resuscitation, but nothing happened.

We got him to the hospital and they worked with him, and finally put him in a crib in a room. He remained there for thirty days before regaining consciousness. That was the beginning of a long and difficult struggle, and over seventy-five hospital stays. Butch never talked again, and did not regain his ability to walk until he was about five years old. The hospital could not discover what was wrong with him. We knew that the extreme heat had something to do with his illness. The baby sitter had gone to the basement and opened the door to the heater and the heat was turned up very high. The specialists who were consulted said he would not live beyond two years. But doctors are just human beings, as fallible as the rest of us, and it was God who was controlling the calendar. Throughout his twenty-two years of life, we were summoned to the hospital at least forty times to see him before he died.

I began to call on God like never before.

We went through trying times with our son. I was only twenty-three years old, a young mother overwhelmed by the responsibility of caring for my sick child. One day I was holding him, and he had his first of many convulsions. It scared me badly. We rushed him to the hospital in an ambulance, where they kept him for ten days. That was the beginning of thousands of convulsions. He had them up to thirty times a day and night.

I turned all of my body, mind, and spirit to the Lord. I knew how to pray because I had prayed all my life. I bombarded Heaven with prayers to let us keep our baby, no matter what condition he was in. There was a multitude of people praying along with us. I took very good care of my little girl and my husband. We thanked the Lord when my baby turned two, for it was a milestone that medical science said he would never pass. When he lived past three, then four, I realized my faith was in the right place.

We purchased special shoes for Butch and he began to pull up and try to walk. His convulsions continued day and night. We put his crib in our room so our daughter would not be disturbed. I learned to sleep so lightly that I could hear a change in my child's breathing. Throughout the night he would have violent grand mal seizures. They would continue through the next day. I had to put compressors on his tongue to keep him from choking. I had to roll the heavy saliva out of his throat to keep him from strangling to death. I tried to take care of him so his daddy, who worked with dangerous machinery, could get his sleep. I also did my best with Pegeen to insure she would have a normal, healthy childhood.

It was suggested that we take our son to Johns Hopkins Hospital. I made three appointments, and we began dipping heavily into our savings. We contacted friends who secured us a room in Baltimore, and John took off from work and drove us there. He stayed one day, and after making sure we were all right, returned home to look after Pegeen. I had to take a taxi to get to Johns Hopkins Hospital. I went with the highest hopes. My faith was at its peak. I said a prayer before every test. The family we were staying with showered us with kindness, and I will be eternally grateful to them.

After ten days, I was called in for a conference. They told me they had discovered the problem, but that there was no medical treatment, and if my son lived long enough, he might outgrow it. The baby had fallen asleep with his head against the heating vent, and he had lapsed into a coma. The specialists told me that the excessive heat had cooked an eighth of his brain. That's why he had lost the ability to speak. He was, by this time, walking quite well, but we had to hold his hands to keep him from falling. I was stunned at this news. I asked them to forward their findings to our family doctor. Our doctor, as well as other people, encouraged us to put him in an institution, but I was determined not to let that happen.

After we returned home, all of my disappointments set in. The doctor told me I could not stand up under the strain, but I continued to take care of my son. My nerves were becoming frayed. I did not neglect my duties, but the demands of the situation were exhausting. One day I fell asleep on the couch. Pegeen was in school, and I thought I had locked the screen door. Something startled me and I woke up immediately. I wasn't used to sleeping soundly. I called little Butch. I couldn't find him anywhere. I was panic stricken. We lived one block from the Delaware River and I feared he may have wandered there. I bolted out of the house and ran down to the river. Out of the corner of my eye, I saw a movement near the top of the water tower. Butch had climbed about seventy steps up. I nearly dropped dead from fright. I made a mad dash, taking the ladder rungs two and three at a time. I grabbed his feet and held on. We were spotted up there and eventually the fire company brought us down.

I began to shake and cry when we got home. That evening Butch went into violent seizures that lasted throughout the night. He was rushed to the hospital where we were told he wouldn't last the night. The last few months had been exhausting, and I lost considerable weight from lack of sleep and loss of appetite. For years, I had had a serious respiratory problem. At times, I had frightening breathing attacks, and I had been advised to travel to Arizona for a different climate. I knew I could not upset my family by uprooting them and moving to Arizona. I kept my condition to myself as much as possible. My breathing condition was aggravated and my total health imperilled.

A few days later, my husband found me on the floor. I had suffered a nervous breakdown. The doctor said I would die or end up in a mental institution if I kept my son. He said I needed a lot of rest. He told us he could get little Butch emergency care in an institution sixty miles away. We didn't have anyone to take care of him. He was almost as tall as I was, and he could run like the wind. We didn't have a fenced yard, so I watched him as carefully as I could, but occasionally he got out of sight. My health was broken; I was rundown and tired much of the time. Finally I collapsed.

One morning, I could not raise myself out of bed. John stayed with me that day. It was then I decided to sign the papers for Butch to be institutionalized. It broke my heart. They wanted to transfer him right from the hospital, but I said no, I would take him. I wanted to see where he would be staying.

The doctor came to meet me. Some of my girlfriends went with me because the situation was too much for John. The doctor put an identification bracelet on Butch. In the compound Butch bolted away and went to play with the other children. I started to chase him, but the doctor stayed me.

"He can't go anywhere," the doctor said, "his every moment is watched." When we left, the doctor said Butch would be all right. "You leave now, it will be easier this way."

I left crying like a baby, went home and broke down completely.

I cannot express the anguish and searing pain that I experienced when I had to leave my son. I can never tell you what I went through, wondering if he were going to receive the special care that I believe I alone could give him. Only a mother under the same circumstances would understand. I wondered if God had forgotten us. Later on in life, I learned to live by the Holy Scripture that says in Romans 8:28 that all things work together for the good of those who love the Lord and are called to His purpose. But, this was now, and I was separated from my little boy who was very, very ill.

Slow Recovery and Growing Hope

I couldn't seem to snap back. My mind and body were used to certain routines, and it was hard to adjust to inactivity. The doctor suggested that after I was sufficiently rested, I should find something to keep my mind and hands occupied. After a few months, I went to work part-time, four hours a day. I decided to go to night school as well, and chose subjects that I was most interested in. I had my own ceramic studio at home. I attended one of the best drama schools in

Philadelphia and acted in "Anna Lucasta," as Blanche, and also in J. B. Priestley's "They Came to a City," as Alice Foster. I played the nurse, Miss Preen, in Kaufman and Hart's "The Man Who Came to Dinner." I even had a walk-on part in the TV drama, "Actions in the Afternoon."

One of the most helpful classes I attended was psychology, for it guided me through the difficult transition I was making. One day, Mary Dee of Station WHAT, in Philadelphia, asked me to come and lend a hand, so I was a Christian disk jockey for a day. It was an exciting opportunity. My son had been away for a year now, and I was trying to learn all I could.

I usually went to visit Butch twice a month, sharing the sixty-mile drive to the institution with my girlfriend. But it was a bad, snow-filled winter, and we hadn't been able to see him in a month. I was overjoyed when the weather broke, and my girlfriend came to visit. She had taken the day off from work, and we caught up on each other's lives on the drive up.

When we arrived, we went to the building where Butch usually stayed, but he wasn't there. I became panicky when the help said they did not know where he was. We went from building to building, but couldn't find him. Before searching out the doctor, we decided to go to the last building, the one where they put the worst cases, the unruly patients, the ones that could not go to the bathroom by themselves or put on their own clothes.

I didn't think my son could possibly be there. I rang the buzzer and an attendant, one of the patients, came to the door. He carried a belt of about thirty big keys. He would not open the outside door. He said he could not let me in. I begged him, but he would not budge. I asked him to let us in the hallway, he could bring the patients out for us to see. When he opened the inner door, my blood nearly froze. There were wild animal screams coming from the hallway. I wanted to run out the door and get in my car, but I was determined to find my child.

My girlfriend backed away screaming, but returned when she saw I was standing firm. The attendant asked how old my son was. I told him he was seven years old. He began to bring children to me. They didn't look human, they were dirty and unkempt. Then he brought another child. There was a hint of recognition from his eyes. In my heart I knew it was Butch, but my mind was in denial.

"That's him," my friend said.

"Oh no!" I said, "My boy is a beautiful, hazel-eyed child. This looks like an animal!" I broke out into tears for this sad little boy.

I reluctantly looked at him again. He wasn't wearing any shoes. He was filthy. There were feces matted in his brown hair. But I knew it was he. I pulled my winter coat off and stooped down and picked him up. They said I couldn't take him home, but I challenged anyone to stop me. I posed a very formidable sight. My girlfriend drove home, and I cuddled that little boy all the way. He had a horrible odor, and I couldn't wait to get him into the bathtub. We had to cut off all his hair because we could not get all of the feces out.

The next day the police came to our home and said I had broken the law. I told them I was going to expose that place for its inhumane treatment to children. They didn't pursue the matter, and we kept our son.

A few weeks later Butch became deathly ill. After two days in the hospital we were called in to see him. It was two o'clock in the morning, and we were told he would not live to see the next day. We had been through this many times before. I called some elders to set up a Prayer Vigil. John and I stayed with our son and prayed all night. He was up and around the next morning.

One of the elders said Oral Roberts was in a town nearby and that I should take my son to see him. We went to the service and it was a beautiful blessing to us. It increased our faith in God. I was determined I was going to keep my child alive.

I went to work for Mrs. G. H. Fenton. This lady and her family and I became dear friends over the years. She was a special kind of person: the givingest person you would want to meet. She became my friend, my confidante, and my benefactor. I could tell her all my problems. She would always listen. She had two beautiful children, a girl, Karen, and a boy, Jack. I used to babysit them.

One day, while burning trash in the Fenton's incinerator, I discovered a magazine article about a specialist in neurology. I read the complete article when I got home. Dr. Wilder Penfield had a neurological hospital in Montreal, Canada, and I was very much interested in his research. I talked it over with my husband, and he wasn't sure if we could afford to engage Dr. Penfield. I wrote a ten-page letter to Dr. Penfield, praying fervently over each word, pouring out my heart. I took the letter to Mrs. Fenton, and she cried. Mrs. Fenton and her husband came to our home that same evening. She told me they owned the largest laundry in Montreal. I was very surprised to hear it. They told us to send the letter airmail and not to worry about finances, they would stand for any amount we needed. They were to come to our financial assistance many times over the years.

We were very optimistic. It looked as if God was answering our prayers. Mrs. Fenton arranged an apartment for us in Montreal. In five weeks, we received correspondence from Canada. Dr. Penfield would see Butch at his earliest convenience. At the present time, he was in Europe where he was the acting physician to royalty. In the meantime, we counted our finances. John was a very proud person and we wanted to pay our own bills. He took a second job to meet expenses. I cooked barbecued pork chops on the weekend and sold them to the various clubs. I opened a little ceramic shop in my home. Our savings had dwindled drastically over the years because of our son's medical bills, but with John's extra work, my work, and some income from the ceramic shop, we did fairly well financially. We saved every penny we could and we had the assurance of help from the Fentons. During the time we waited for our son's appointment in Canada, our lives went up and down. We decided our home was too small. We needed a large yard with fencing all around so we could let Butch play unattended. We found a home on a corner with a huge yard and three big trees, and we purchased the home with a substantial down payment, so our monthly mortgage payments were small. We moved in immediately.

I felt something was missing from our family, so we purchased a large black dog for our son and called him Champ. We also bought a smaller variety for our daughter, Pegeen. We called him Rex. Those dogs protected our children and home for many years, and they brought us much joy. Butch loved the river, he was drawn toward it, and we were afraid for him. Any time he left the yard, Rex and Champ would follow him. They actually saved his life several times. One day I got a letter from the Montreal Neurological Institute. They gave us an appointment one month ahead. With everyone praying for our son, we prepared to go to Canada. Mr. and Mrs. Fenton gave us several letters assuring officials that we would not become a burden in Montreal.

Montreal

The temperature was very hot when we left home. My son could not talk, but he would make loud sounds when he became excited. We were told to keep him quiet on the train. If the officials knew his condition, we could have trouble crossing the border. I had

1,500 dollars that my husband had given me. My niece went with us to help out. With a prayer in my heart, we left for Canada.

We did very well until we were ready to exit the train in Montreal. Butch, I suppose, was very excited because he gave out a terrible yell. The conductors made us sit down. They questioned me about my son. They wanted to see Dr. Penfield's letter. We had to show them our money as well. I showed them a letter from Mr. and Mrs. Jack Fenton, which stated that the general manager of the laundry would be there at the station to meet us. They had the manager paged, and this very business-like man came to where we were sitting. He introduced himself as Mr. Swales, showed the conductor a card, and took us off the train. He had a black minister, Rev. Fisher, with him, a humble man.

In a large black car they accompanied us to a nice apartment. The landlord, a smiling African woman, fixed us a splendid lunch. The minister remained with us. He was a devout Christian man willing to help us in any way he could. I really appreciated it. There was a knock at the door, and the minister opened it. There stood Mr. Swales and two men with a small refrigerator and several bags of food. They showed me a cook stove in the hall. They also brought me a fan because the temperature was over 100 degrees. The local papers had reported that several people had died from the heat. I was quite concerned because of my respiratory problems. Thank God the fan worked so well.

That night I knelt in prayer and thanked God that my son hadn't had any seizures in quite some time. We arose early the next morning so we could get to our first appointment. When we went to the hall to heat water for tea, I met some of the other tenants. The apartment building housed a German family, a Romanian family, and a Malaysian family. It was a very interesting melting pot living under one roof. No one knew each other's language, but I am a very friendly, outgoing person, and we managed to communicate. Everyone else I met spoke French, which was a real challenge for me.

We went with Rev. Fisher in a taxi to the Institute. Dr. Penfield received us immediately. He had reviewed all of Butch's hospital and doctor's reports. He took time to talk to me thoroughly and set up three appointments for Butch to be examined. He apologized that it took five years to see my son. He said he never took a patient on the mother's request—only a doctor could make an appointment—but my ten-page letter had touched his heart. After reading it, he said he couldn't do anything else but respond. He was also the doctor to the Dionne quintuplets.

That afternoon we went sightseeing in the taxi. We went to see the Shrine of Saint Joseph. It was an awesome sight. The church had such a beautiful ethereal atmosphere, and the larger than life statues took my breath away. I cried like a baby; there were so many things to see. The day was very hot, and I later learned that many people had suffered from sunstroke. We were exhausted, so we drove back to the apartment and remained indoors for the rest of the day. I roamed the halls and met some other mothers. It was funny as we tried to communicate with one another. The German lady took my hand and led me to her apartment. She had a husband, a son, and two daughters. They showed me pictures, and we laughed quite a lot. Laughter took the place of talking.

We arose early the next day. The temperature remained over one hundred. I noticed that my son was somewhat listless this morning. Rev. Fisher would not be with us today, so we were on our own. After the appointment, we decided to walk around. I had expressed the desire to see some churches, and Rev. Fisher had given me a list. It was quite warm and I was having a problem breathing. We came to one of the more famous streets in Montreal, Rue Madelaine, busy with people and cars. That street is the Rodeo Drive of Montreal. As we crossed, Butch's body suddenly began to convulse. He was having a seizure. He fell helpless in the middle of the street. I couldn't carry him because he was too big. The cars and taxis were swerving all around us. In a panic, I lay flat on top of my son, as if my being there could protect him. The police came and stopped traffic. I could hear people saying, "Drunk! Drunk!" I stopped my praying and looked up. "No! No!" I shouted, "He's ill!" All I could hear was the jangle of incomprehensible French. The crowd was tremendous. Oh! The frustration of not being able to communicate. I reached in my purse and gave the police the paper with Doctor Penfield's name on it. He recognized it. He stooped and picked up Butch. He placed us in a cab and told the driver, in French, to take us to the hospital. I thanked the officer and prayed for him.

At the hospital, Butch was given first aid, and after a two-hour rest, we called the taxi and returned home. I was exhausted. I turned the fan on and we rested until dinner. The temperature was 103 degrees. Butch was quiet and subdued the rest of the evening. The German and Romanian ladies came to visit. I showed them pictures and told them about Butch. We all had a good cry. Language is no barrier when mothers talk about their children.

During the night I noticed a change in the atmosphere. I turned the fan off, and about four o'clock in the morning I heard something hitting the window. I looked out, and was astonished to find it snowing. By morning the streets and homes were covered with ice and snow. It was beautiful yet deadly. We could not venture outside.

I decided to have a party that evening in our apartment. After breakfast, I went from door to door. I got my message across by drawing pictures and using my hands, taking a guitar and strumming it, pointing to the time and putting a pot on the stove and walking to the door with it. We laughed a lot. I went home and barbequed all of my pork chops and hamburger. I made macaroni salad and punch and waited for evening. It was quite a surprise to see everyone come with pots and pans, guitar and violin. The landlord came, all six feet four of her! She brought her man friend, a little five feet two Frenchman. Now that was a sight!

We ate, sang, danced, and had a delightful time. All of the tenants in the apartment were displaced from their respective countries, and it was this that bound us together. It seemed as if we knew each other all of our lives. We partied until two o'clock in the morning. Unfortunately, Butch became very excited and had several seizures. It was pitiful. We all had a good cry before everyone left.

We arrived at the hospital for Butch's final appointment. Dr. Penfield sent Butch and my niece into another room while we had our conference. He told me what the examinations showed. It was just like the report I received when I took him to Johns Hopkins Hospital in Baltimore. Then, Dr. Penfield told me something cruelly ironic. He could have helped my son five years ago, but now there was nothing he could do. It was five years ago that I first discovered the article on Dr. Penfield and wrote for an appointment. Now here he was telling me it was too late. I was stunned. The doctor explained that Butch was going to grow to be about six feet five inches tall. Eventually he would have to be institutionalized because he was going to become extremely hyper and unmanageable. I thanked the doctor for his time and left.

Before I left the hospital, I received the bill, and it was a staggering amount. I could never pay that amount. The bill said "Paid In Full." It had been paid by the laundry. I really thanked God for my dear friends, Mr. and Mrs. Fenton. I felt an urge to return to New Jersey even though I had planned to stay another week. I was numb going back to our room. My head was getting stuffy. The rest of the day passed in a haze.

I called Mr. Swales and told him my plans. We would leave the next day if we could get a train out. He told me not to worry, he would take care of it. I said goodbye to all my neighbors. Everyone came to see me off, and we took a lot of pictures. Mr. Swales came with Rev. Fisher to take us to the station. I thanked everyone and told them God was going to bless them for their kindness and support.

Suicide Attempt

By the time we were settled on the train, I was feeling quite ill. I fed my son when we arrived home and made calls to my sisters. Then I locked all the doors and fell unconscious to the floor.

I came to in the emergency ward.

When I hadn't answered the front door, my sisters had looked through the window. They broke in and called my husband. They took me to the hospital, burning up with fever, almost incoherent. The weather in Canada and the disappointment in the outcome of the visit was more than I could take, and it took its toll on my weakened body. I nearly had bronchitis and was on the verge of another breakdown.

The days that followed were hazy and indistinct. God knew I needed a good physical and mental rest. The first Saturday after I left the hospital, the whole clan came to our home to hear about our trip to Canada. My sisters brought covered dishes, and we had a good time. We hadn't gotten together in a long time. Our families had gotten so big.

Butch was still having very bad seizures. They were getting worse every day. He had contracted a fever, and he had seizures for two days. I had not slept in nearly thirty hours. I sent John off to work and Pegeen off to school. I told my husband I slept during the day, but I didn't. I was in a fog. I cooked and cleaned. I bathed and changed Butch until I thought I would drop. "If only someone would come and sit by his bed," I thought, "so I could get some rest." But everyone was frightened of my son's seizures. I could understand it, because they were horrible to see. I had to keep awake to save him from choking to death on his tongue. Afterward, his body was coma-locked, immobile. After dealing with over fifty seizures without sleep, I lost

97

control of my faculties. I felt dizzy before each siege. I lost all reasoning.

I decided it was time to bring it to an end. I went to the table and got his new bottle of phenobarbital and dilantin. I divided the pills into two piles, about forty pills each. I wasn't in my right mind. Lack of sleep and stress had pushed me over the edge. I went to Butch and tried to force his mouth open. After nearly ten hours in a coma, he opened his eyes, and his gaze spoke to me, "Don't do it, Mom." He hadn't talked since his first attack.

I pried his mouth open and just as I was putting the pills in, something slapped me halfway across the room. The pills scattered every which way. I lay on the floor. I felt another being in that room, yet there was no one there but Butch and I. Then I realized the phone was ringing. It was a loud and persistent ring. I crawled down the hall and picked up the receiver. I was incoherent. All I could say was, "I've killed my son." I heard my door opening downstairs. The police and ambulance attendants ran upstairs calling me. A policeman took the phone and said, "All right. We're here." They saw the pills on the floor. They read both bottles, and counted the pills. Thank God they were all accounted for.

I was hyperventilating, and they gave me oxygen. They attended me until I was stable. I asked them what they were doing here. The call was from the institution, the doctor telling me that they had an opening if I wanted to put Butch there. It was an immediate opening, and when I said I had killed my son, they held me on the line until they could contact the police. The doctor who called was sixty miles away. The Lord works in mysterious ways.

A few days later, after a lot of soul searching, we committed our son to the institution. I got a lot of rest, but I worried about him. I couldn't seem to stop worrying. I was very rundown. John had to take me to the doctor. The doctor ran some tests and afterward, to my surprise, told me I was pregnant. I was amazed because I had been told I could not have another baby. We were shocked, but very happy.

In the meantime, we were constantly called to the hospital to see our son "for the last time." It was a long trip. The doctors and nurses told me to give him up, to let him go because he was suffering. I was still attending all Revival Healing Services and staying in constant prayer. I would put my mouth to my son's unconscious ear and pray, sometimes all night. He would open his eyes, and we would go home. It happened again and again. He kept snapping out of it, and I would have to brace myself and wait for the next "last time."

Early one morning, all the sisters were called to the hospital. Our Papa had suffered a major stroke and was on the critical list. Our stepmother didn't want us to see him, but we paid no attention to her. He was hospitalized for a week before he was taken off the critical list. After a few more days, the doctor said he could come home. Three of the sisters went to pick him up. As Papa stooped down to put his shoes on, he dropped dead. It was a great shock. We went to pieces. We had a very large funeral for Papa, and we have missed him very much. He and Mama were special parents.

I learned at this time that the three youngest sisters were all expecting, each of us one month apart. We anxiously awaited our babies. Nell delivered her third child, and then Vi delivered her baby. I was in the choir on a Sunday morning singing when my first labor pains started. Twenty-four hours later, I gave birth to a darling little boy, whom we named Donald Bruce. We were ecstatic. Pegeen, our daughter, really loved her new baby brother.

Passing

I joined the NAACP in the 1960s. There was so much prejudice and injustice in the world. In the South, Martin Luther King, Jr. was coming into prominence, and he was leading peaceful marches. We had a young, dynamic president of our NAACP of South Jersey, Willie James. I was active in sit-ins and demonstrations all over the county. We found families held on farms working in slave conditions, their children (as many as nine) suffering from malnutrition. No one could read or write. We found housing and jobs and schools for some of them, and we were glad when they prospered. Through demontrations, we integrated several major department stores in the county. We fought to get one of the biggest developments integrated. I helped to coordinate the Burlington County march on Washington. It was one of the most glorious, inspiring events in my life. I went to Chicago as an NAACP delegate and helped to demonstrate at the Morris Hotel to have the black jockey statue removed from the front of it. We were successful.

There were so many wonderful history-making events that we were part of. I was chosen many times to represent the organization during speaking engagements. Our president, Willie James, and many members of our branch, were instrumental in getting the Burlington

County Community Action in our area. I was very proud to be part of all of it.

I was very busy, but I took very good care of my family. After we were able to get black families into the large development in Willingboro, New Jersey, there were quite a few demonstrations against us, but we all rallied around the black homes. Things kind of cooled off. At this time, my little boy Donald Bruce was growing nicely. We really enjoyed him.

At home, I held a prayer shut-in for five days. I had done it several times in the past. During the shut-in, you prayed and communed with God. You didn't eat or answer the phone. It was hard because I still had to cook and take care of the family. Two days after I went off the shut-in, I heard a voice in my sleep. It sounded like my son Butch. The voice said, "Good-bye Mama. I'm going home. I love you."

Butch was sixty miles away and he could not talk, but I heard his voice as plain as day. I said, "Good-bye son. I'll see you one day. I love you."

I turned the light on and looked at the clock. It was 3:30AM. I was at peace. I knew my son had finally passed away. My husband sat up and asked, "What's the matter?"

"Butch told me good-bye," I said. "He just died."

John said, "Hush, and go back to sleep."

"They are going to call us soon."

John was very nervous. He thought I had gone off of my rocker. He sat up and lit a cigarette. The phone rang and he began to tremble. He said, "You answer it."

"No, you answer it. I know who it is and what they will say."
John slowly picked up the phone and answered it. He looked at me with wide eyes. Then he said, "What time?"

I said, "3:30," and he was so stunned he hung the phone up and turned to me. "You were right. It was 3:30."

I believe the good Lord let me hear his voice one more time, and I've always thanked Him for that privilege.

Our son had developed boils all over his body, and they had eaten up his tissues. The embalming fluid could not stay in his body after thirty-six hours, so we rushed to hold his funeral. It was very sad, but God sustained us. I wrote a poem for him and it was read at the funeral. The hurt of losing a child was terrible, but thank God time heals all hurts, and we know he would not suffer any more. My son, John, Jr., died in July 1966 at twenty-two years of age.

To My Beloved Son

My son, you've gone home to your father
Where no sorrow, suffering or pain
Can ever be present to haunt you,
And only memories remain.

You suffered long and patiently,
You never once complained.
It broke my heart to see you
But I did again, again, and again.

I did the best I could for you,
I did not want you to leave,
But God has always promised
All our sorrows to relieve.
Sleep on my beautiful,
You know I loved you so.
I know you have found happiness
In the place we all must go.

Forgive me for anything I forgot
In proving my love for you.
Goodbye my beautiful baby,
For I bid you a Heavenly adieu.

Love, Mommy

Five sisters, left to right: Nell, the author,
Vivian on her 50th wedding anniversary, Lucy, and Nina.

Left to right: Dorothy Scott (relative), Peggy Morris Evans,
Eduardo Hernandez (groom), Kimberly Morris Hernandez (bride),
the author, and Donald Bruce Morris

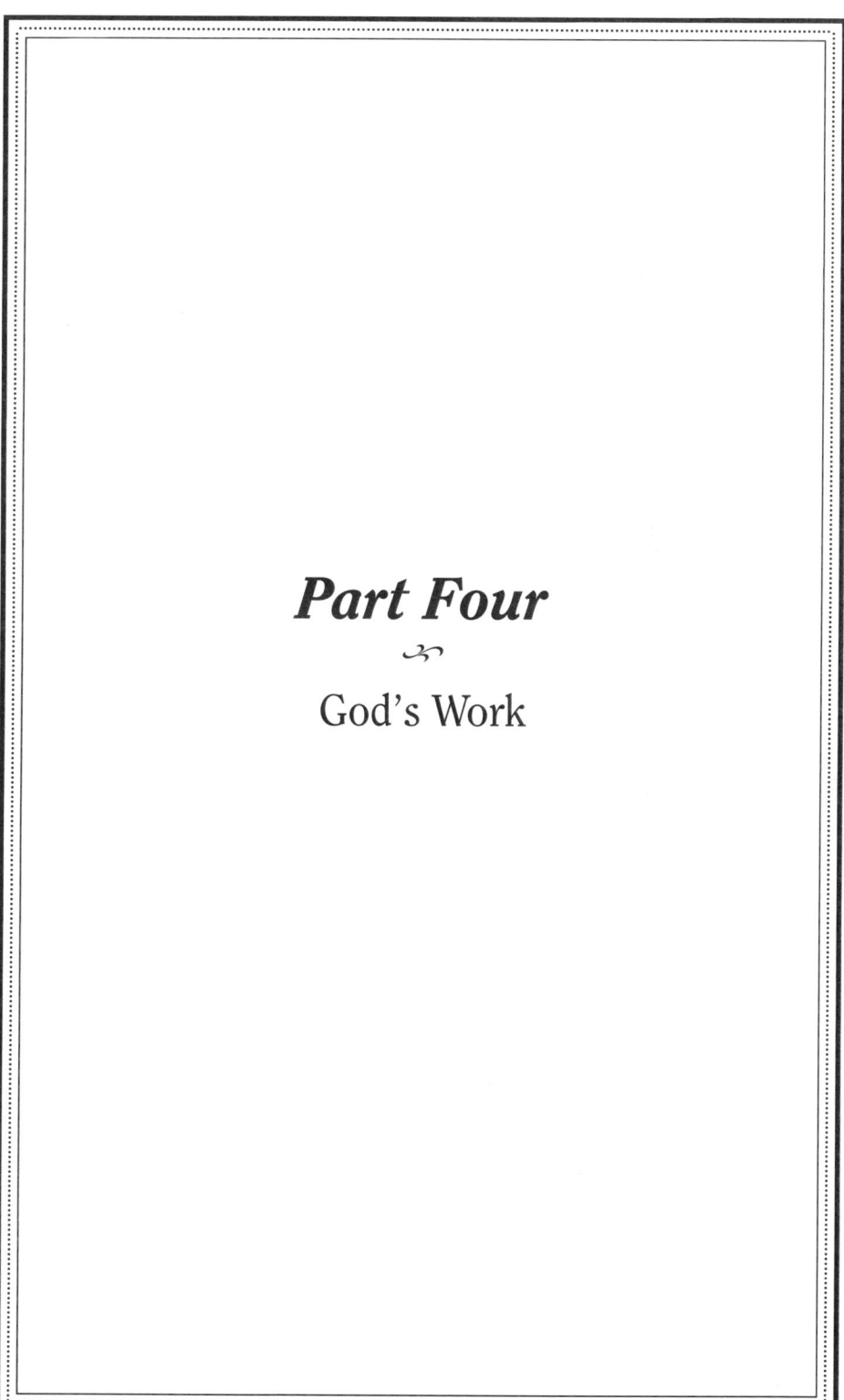

Part Four

God's Work

The author officiates at a Christening in Brooklyn.

Slowly, we settled back into a routine, and we thanked God we had another child to love. I again became active in the church. I delighted in writing and performing in religious dramas. I went to visit my old Christian friend, Mrs. Jamison, in Riverside. We talked a long time and prayed all afternoon. Before I left she told me that God was calling me to do His work. He had called me years ago, but I had been too busy to hear His voice, and now with my son gone, there was nothing to stop me from answering His call. My soul and spirit went into denial at what she was saying.

For a while, it seemed as if time had grown wings and taken flight. Pegeen had finished high school and was engaged to be married. The wedding was taking up all of my time, and my mind was off what Mrs. Jamison had told me. In my free hours, I was writing sermons, drama, and poetry. It seemed as if there weren't enough time in the day to do all I wanted to do. I gave no time to my calling as Pegeen's wedding became an obsession. Pegeen finally picked her wedding party of cousins and friends. She and I had a most delightful time picking her wedding dress. On the morning of her wedding it rained cats and dogs. She was so upset. I told her not to worry because God wanted her to have a pretty, sunny day for her wedding. She was to be married at three o'clock in the afternoon. At twelve o'clock, the sun came out and at two o'clock it was as if it hadn't rained at all. I wondered why or how I had prophesized this. She became Mrs. Leonard Evans at three o'clock—a handsome couple—and we loved them both so much.

Time passed on. I found out I was getting ready to have another baby. Nell and Vi told me they were expecting as well. We three sisters got a lot of teasing. We grew fat together. Again, we delivered one month apart. I enjoyed carrying the baby. Amazingly, I was in the choir when labor started in the very same seat where it started with my last child. After giving birth to a beautiful little girl, Kimberly Diahne, I decided to change my seat in that choir.

We had a most delightful time with our two little children. We would have been very lonely without our two adorable children. Pegeen was married and living in their home. Our first baby had long since gone on to be with the Lord. We thanked God frequently for those last two. But my health was failing.

My Conversion

I tried to stay very busy in civic as well as church work, but my respiratory problems were getting worse. For years, I had a chronic cough and occasional heavy nose bleeds. Now, it seemed as if my whole body was about to give out. I made two trips to the hospital to have lumps removed from my breast. The doctors thought each time they were cancerous. They were not, thank God. A few months later, I was returned to the hospital with acute pain. The test showed a bad hiatal hernia and an infected gall bladder, which they wanted to remove. I refused to have the operation. I still have my gall bladder and hernia.

My health was up and down. I began to cough continuously, and suffered excruciating stomach pains. I began to lose weight rapidly and was coughing up great chunks of flesh. The doctors never gave me a direct answer to my condition. I began to think the worst. I was taking ten to fifteen pills a day and one bottle of cough syrup every two days. I was scared to death that I was dying. I was fainting at least three to four times a day.

During my illness, my sister Lucy would come and take care of our children and help out. One day I was feeling quite well, so I thought I would go visit the superintendent of our Sunday School. I was his assistant. He was very ill with terminal cancer. I went with a friend of mine. After visiting for awhile, he asked me to get his medicine off the bureau. I went to get it, and I nearly died from fright. Three bottles of his medicine were identical to mine. I didn't stay long after that. I was completely devastated.

I was going downhill fast. One evening, quite late, Pegeen came to the house. She had borrowed my car to go to a revival in another town. She was always a pretty girl, but this time there was a glow about her that was almost ethereal. She had a light in her face that made tears come to my eyes. I had never seen anyone as beautiful as she was that moment standing in front of me. She came and hugged me. There was something different in her touch. I thought it was because she knew I had cancer and I was dying. She said, "Mama, I have a message for you."

"From whom?"

"The Holy Ghost," she said. "You are to come to the revival tomorrow." She began to tell me her experience. She had been baptized in the Holy Spirit. I was too sick to be bothered, and I finally got her to go home. I went outside and began to walk, just walking up and down the river until three o'clock in the morning. I could not settle down. I went home and went to bed and coughed all night. I got up the next morning and took care of my duties, and I began to pray, but I couldn't find peace in my prayer. That evening, my daughter and some friends of mine came and reminded me of the message the Holy Spirit had sent. I told them I didn't feel like going. They didn't pressure me.

Afterward, my daughter came to the house again and said to me, "The Holy Spirit said you are to come to the revival."

When she left, I spent another restless night. I was functioning in a haze of pain. I hurt so bad. I had two very bad coughing spells. Not only did flesh and pus come up, but I began to bleed from my stomach. I tried catching the hunks of flesh, thinking with my numb brain that I could save my stomach that way. It was horrible. I refused to go to the doctor or hospital. I tried staying on my feet and hiding my condition from my family, but I was so sick.

I hadn't slept all night. I was very weak from coughing and my anemic condition. I managed to hide my condition from John that morning. I sent him off to work with a good breakfast and the children off to school. John made a remark about my loss of weight. As I stood washing dishes, the phone rang. It was my hairdresser, a very devout lady who was one of my Christian mothers. She said she had a message for me but did not understand it. She said, "The Holy Ghost sent for you twice and this will be the last time."

I told her about the messages my daughter had brought.

She said, "Don't eat anything today," and told me to go into prayer for the rest of the day.

With Pegeen and my girlfriend, Lou, I went to the revival. It was held in the beautiful Black Holiness Church. I had never seen such radiant black or white faces. I believe the faces of the congregation could have lit up the world. The choir was singing, "I'm running for my life," and I realized that was what I was doing. The faces of the minister and his associate minister were beautiful.

I took an aisle seat. Soon after the devotionals, the guest minister was introduced. I had heard of this great woman of God, but I had never seen her. As she took her place at the pulpit, I nearly fainted at the sight of her countenance. She was engulfed in a beautiful glow. It was as if I were again that little four-year-old who stood on the corner listening to the woman preach about the Holy Ghost. The minister, Mother Mildred Water Spain, looked like an angel in her white robe. When the revivalist began to talk, I was enraptured. After greeting everyone, she chose her text, Psalm One Hundred Sixteen, the twelfth verse: "What shall I render unto the Lord for all His benefits toward me?" The words of the twelfth verse were like a neon light in my mind.

As she began to preach, I thought of all the things the Lord had done for me. He had let me keep my son for twenty-two years when medical science said it was impossible. He had given me two more children after I was told I could have no more. I thought of how the Lord had made it possible for us to buy a large home on a corner with a yard for our son to be safe in. My mind went to my illnesses and the length of time He had let me live, and then, sitting there, I thought, "What have I given the Lord?" I didn't have time. I had to take care of my son. I had to do this and that, but never too much for the Lord. I didn't hear the rest of the sermon, I was crying so hard.

Mother Spain announced the altar call. They tell me I shot up to the altar and fell on my knees. I began to pray and ask forgiveness of the Lord. I told Him I realized I was dying, but with the life I had left I wanted to do His work. I began to sway back and forth. I felt arms laying me on the floor. Something touched the top of my head. It felt like warm blood being poured into my head, coursing down through my whole body. I could feel strength and, while slain in the Spirit, saw this beautiful figure standing over me. Two hands reached into my stomach and chest and pulled out masses of bloody flesh. I could feel it being pulled lovingly out of my body. I felt so good, I wanted to go home to be with the Lord right then. Lying there, I was transported back to the time I was a sixth grader at Mrs. Jamison's home. We had been praying, and she laid her hands on me, and I fell on her floor and began to speak strange words. I was speaking a beautiful language lying on the floor of the church. I had been operated on by the Supreme Physician Himself. He gave me a new blood transfusion, and from that day on, I've never had to have another.

I sat up in a daze, but I was happy. I felt as if I had died and gone to Heaven. I realized the old me had died, and now I was reborn. I stood up and I realized that the sickness I went to church with, all that weak dizziness, was gone. It was as if this body that I now inhabited was not the same body I left home with. When I realized what had happened, the joy and the love of My Lord and Savior were enormous. I wanted to tell Him so much. My tongue could not utter the words. I began to speak in glossallalia and words of love came in different tongues. They came and came. I have never been the same person from that moment on.

I was told later that all the ministers were standing around me. Pegeen and my girlfriend Louise Jackson were praying for me. They had had that great experience a few days before, and they shared in my joy. When we left the church that night. I was still on a most glorious high.

My husband noticed as soon as I returned home that something wonderful had happened. I told him I would talk to him later. I went to bed. I couldn't sleep. I was on cloud nine, ten, eleven, and twelve. John came to bed, and after he went to sleep, the joy of my experience overcame me, and I began to speak in that heavenly tongue. My husband woke up, and he respected what was happening even though he was somewhat bewildered by it all. I decided to tell him all about it when he came home from work the next day. He was very happy for me, and he always showed me the utmost respect.

At my own church, I tried to explain what had happened, but I was scorned and treated like a leper. My pastor hurt me so bad. He tried to get me to renounce what had happened to me. Members of the board and members of my family (other than John and Pegeen) did not support me, and they caused me to shed many tears.

I lost quite a few friends. Some called me and told me to "stop that foolishness." One relative told me she was tired of her sister being called a fool, and that I had lost my mind. Some of the neighbor's children would get in front of my house and mock the Holy Spirit by acting like they were dancing and speaking in tongues. In later years, every one of them eventually came to me for prayer or guidance. In spite of all of the trials and tribulations, I was happy. Yes, I lost a lot of friends when I was baptized in the Holy Spirit, but the Lord gave me many more friends.

I turned my life over to Jesus. The Lord sent me some beautiful saints. I went to all kinds of revivals. I attended two Bible schools. The Scripture was coming alive to me in a most miraculous way. I met some of the most dynamic ministers in the world: Jack Cole, Oral Roberts, Robert Schambach, Thea Jones, Mother Daleney, Rev. Doris Broadway, Rev. Alvin Jackson, and A. A. Allen. Most of the ministers prayed for me and my family and I owe them all so very much. It was wonderful. Every day was so rich, I could hardly stand it. Mother Mildred Water Spain who preached at my conversion became very dear to me. She began to visit me and to keep in close contact. She was considered a powerhouse in the religious field. And I traveled with a number of beautiful ministers and pastors. They taught me a lot.

Mother Spain came to me about two years after my conversion and told me she wanted me to go to Philadelphia to enter a shut-in. The church was, and still is, one of the biggest churches in Philadelphia, Deliverance Evangelistic Center. Pastor Benjamin Smith was, and still is, a dynamo. He became a dear friend for all these years, and I thank God for him. My first shut-in was for seven days without eating; an immersion in prayer and meditation. The experience was awesome. I had the privilege of seeing a vision. When I came out of that shut-in after seven days, the world looked so beautiful and clean. I was told by the evangelist to stay in constant prayer and to study the Bible, which I did.

I studied at least six hours every day.

The days rolled by. I was called on to do dramatic readings and preside at different services. My family traveled with me, and our family was very happy. One night while in bed, I heard a voice saying, "You do not have any excuse not to do what I have called you to do. Your son is with Me now. I need you to come into My service. You are to carry My Word. I have prepared you to preach My Word." I looked around the bedroom, I was so frightened. I didn't know what to do.

I went into the hall and looked. There was no one there. I went into my little girl's room. I had the vaporizer on because she had a cold. In a daze, I took the center tube that holds the electric wires to heat the water. It was wet, and when I grabbed it, I was knocked to the floor. There was a brilliant light in the room. It was so bright it nearly blinded me. I lay there for quite some time. I saw that I had the electrode still in my hands. I tried to turn it loose, but I couldn't. I continued to lay in the light. It didn't hurt. I took the bottom of my nightgown and reached over and yanked it out of my hand. The bottom of my nightgown was scorched, but I did not have a single mark on me.

It seemed as if there were an enormous figure in the room, and as I looked, it disappeared, but the bright light remained. After some time passed, I realized I had been electrocuted, but I was still alive. I heard a voice from my childhood telling my Mama that I was going to be sickly all my life and many things were going to happen to me, good and bad. As I lay there, I began to think on the things that had happened to me so far, and there were many. I came to the conclusion the Good Lord wasn't through with me yet.

I finally got off the floor in the morning. The light had disappeared. I don't know how I functioned that day. I was glad John was going to work and the children off to school. I called Mother Swain, the evangelist who preached at my conversion. I told her what had happened during the night. She said she had been led to get out of her bed to pray for me last night. I asked her, "What time was it?" When she told me, I told her it was during the time I was electrocuted. I believe her prayers cut off death from me. I told her about the voice and message. She said she knew I had been called into the ministry. I didn't want to accept it. I went and asked my pastor to talk to me. I told him what had been happening to me for a long time. It was over two years since my baptizing in the Holy Spirit. He hadn't been so nice to me, and he and the Board of Deacons, except for two of them, had caused me to shed many tears. I was a little reluctant to go to him, but I wanted to show him that respect. Well, the advice he gave me really threw me. He said I was losing my mind, and I had better be careful or I would end up in a mental hospital. I came away from that meeting feeling very sorry for him.

I told my husband and children and friends I was called into the ministry to preach, but I wasn't going to pursue it until I was sure it was God calling me. I didn't want to make any mistakes. They said I had their support. I needed time to contemplate. I needed a change of scene to help sort things out, so I decided to go back to work. I wanted to get away from my surroundings for a while.

I found a very nice job in the country, where I went to work twice a week. The lady very seldom left the house. She enjoyed fixing things in her home. We spent many a delightful time while there. She became a very good friend of mine.

After being with her for about three months, I was home one evening, reading my Bible. I had a very strong feeling of anticipation. After finishing reading, I went to bed. I have always had very big dreams. That night, I dreamed as I had before and asked the Lord to verify by sign or word what he had told me to do. I just wanted to hear from Him to be very sure. In my dream that night, I was at work and a knock came at the door. It so happened that my boss had to go to the dentist to have root canal surgery. I answered the door, and there stood a young black priest. He said he was lost and wanted to know how to get to the Catholic church. He said, "I have come this way and I've never been lost before." I did something I usually don't do; I invited him in and gave him a cool glass of lemonade because it was quite hot that day. He introduced himself. He said he was from Africa and had been coming here for four years. I introduced myself, and we began talking.

I awoke the next morning and worked around my home. I didn't have to go to work until the next day. I called two of my girlfriends and one of my advisers and told them my dream. We didn't know what to make of it. My adviser told me she felt it was a message, but she didn't know what it was. I prayed and asked God to reveal to me what it meant. I always prayed over my dreams so I could be enlightened as to what they meant. I pondered on the dream all day while doing my work.

My husband and children came home. We had dinner, and we visited my sisters. They said it was time to renew our get-togethers as we used to. Our sister Odell had gone to New York to live a few years back, and much to our sorrow had passed away. So now we were down to five sisters. We decided to meet at my home on Saturday for a cookout.

I went to work the next day. I was quite nervous, as if I were expecting something to happen, but nothing happened. All week it was as if something were going to happen. I couldn't stop crying.

Anticipating our family cookout finally relieved my anxiety, and I put aside my dream of the black priest. When Saturday came, we had a terrific cookout. We had a whole pig on the spit. We had crabs, potato salad, corn on the cob, corn bread, and collard greens. We had the time of our lives. We all had enough children among us to fill our yard. It was nice to watch them play together, much as we had when we were young. Afterward, we sat around telling jokes at each other's expense. We really missed Odell, because she was usually the instigator of the jokes. This time, Nell proved to be a good substitute.

She began with a story that involved all of the sisters. One Sunday we, Nina, Lucy, Nell, and I, went to visit Odell in New York

City. About a month before, we all had gone to a second-hand fur store and we purchased second-hand furs. We were dressed to kill when we caught the train to New York. We had a ball on the train, laughing and joking.

Odell met us at the station in New York. We walked around for a while really strutting our stuff. Odell said we all really looked like we were rich. Well, we really smiled at that. All of us was rather tall and thin, sort of regal. Odell took us downstairs to get the subway. There weren't any seats for Odell, Lucy, and Nina. Nell and I sat down. Lucy leaned back on the wall of the train. She decided to move and when she did, the eyes of the other passengers were glued to the white wall of the train. Finally, Lucy and Odell turned and looked at the wall. Nina, Nell, and Odell gave a shriek that you could have heard a mile away.

Finally, when Lucy turned around, we realized what had happened while she was leaning against the wall. All of the fur clung to the wall of the train, and the coat was bare of fur in the back. We looked at the wall and the outline of her back was on the wall. It was black fur, and it was moving back and forth as if it were alive. Odell and Nell were screaming. I was trying to be dignified about it, but finally I collapsed into laughter as well. We laughed so hard everyone began to laugh until the whole car was howling. It was really funny. Lucy was still trying to play it cool. Finally she couldn't help but join in laughing. Every time she went near the wall, it snatched the fur off her coat. You should have seen the rest of us when it came time to get off the train. We walked so proud with our heads up high and our arms in front of us so we were sure the wall was not going to snatch our fur coats.

We were just getting back our composure when Odell looked at Lucy and said, "Lucy, you looked like a hen that's molting!" We were laughing so hard we had to sit on the steps to get our senses together. We had a great time at Odell's apartment. Lucy asked Odell for her largest scarf. When we got ready to leave to come home, she put her fur coat on backward, and put the scarf on and draped it down the front. It didn't look too bad. We were so careful on the subway coming back it was really funny. Lucy made sure she sat down; in fact, we all did. When we got on the subway, Odell stuck her head in the door and said as loud as she could, "Walls, don't you dare touch my sisters' coats!" We tried to act dignified and ignored her, but to this very day when we all get together, we still can laugh over the episode.

Well, the cookout came to an end. We all realized how close our family had been and wanted the same for our children.

About a week after I had the dream about the black priest, I was at home in a shut-in. I had been praying and fasting for three days. A very devout Christian minister friend of ours came to the house, and he said he had been thinking very much about me. He told me he had heard that I was called into the ministry, and he said he knew for a long time that the Lord had called me. He said, "When I was teaching you in my class, I knew it, but I wanted you to realize it. The Lord is getting ready to manifest Himself to you in a most profound way, so I came to tell you to be prepared, because I don't know in what way He is going to do it." I said, "Reverend, even though I am in a consecrated shut-in, it seems as if I am running for my life. I am so restless. I'm tired of running away. I've been in denial ever since God called me, and I know I was divinely called, but it seems as if I am waiting for a more profound proof. I certainly hope God will send me the answer soon."

I was led off my shut-in after the fourth day. The next day, I was sitting on our porch after dinner. The children were out with friends. Several people stopped by to sit a while. A few minutes passed while we were talking. After a while, we heard all of this loud cussing and screaming drawing near. We looked and saw a woman who lived in town. She had about twenty people with her. She had the reputation of being bad. I had witnessed to her, but to no avail. She opened my gate rather violently and came on my porch and with a screaming voice and hands on her hips, face in my face, she began to tell me she came to beat and kick my a— because my son beat her son up so she was going to beat me up and then find my son and beat his a—. I had a smile on my face and I told her in the sweetest voice I had, "I love you and Jesus loves you too." I said, "Don't scream so loud, I love you too much to see you hurt yourself. If my son has done wrong, I will punish him." She kept right on cussing. I was led to take her in my arms and hold her real tight. The people were trying to egg her on to fight me, but I talked love to her and she began to cry. My quiet voice calmed her down, and she moved away from me and could hardly look me in the face. She apologized to me and turned to go and a switchblade knife fell out of her pocket.

The crowd was so disappointed and stunned at the outcome. They came to see a fight, and if the Holy Spirit hadn't taken over, it could have been disastrous. That lady and part of that crowd are saved today and working in church. Over the years, Satan sent two more ladies to fight me. They soon found out the fight doesn't belong to me, it belongs to the Lord. He fights my battles, and He has always fought them. I thanked The Lord she did not come at me six or seven years earlier.

I was sorry for the spectacle that was created, but thank God it turned out as it did. I continued being very restless. I couldn't seem to find any peace. I was really running for my life. I was truly miserable. I was still working out in the country, where it was quite a pleasure because it was so peaceful and quiet. About 10 AM one day, the lady of the house told me she had to go to the dentist after lunch. I was quite shocked because she very seldom went out while I was there. I was doubly shocked when I remembered my dream a few nights back. In my dream, she had to go to the dentist and have root canal work. The dream was on my mind all morning.

After we had lunch she left, and I was ironing. It was about two o'clock. There was a knock on the screen door. That was also unusual because in the country, visitors were few. As I went to the door, I nearly dropped from fright, for standing at the screen door was a young black priest. I proceeded to the door and opened it. I don't usually let strangers in, but he didn't seem like a stranger. I recognized him from my dream. He asked directions to the Catholic church in a town about two miles down the road. He said he did not know how he got lost because he had been traveling that road for five years and had never gotten lost. He said something seemed to have happened when he got to that house.

I didn't tell him my dream yet. I invited him to sit down and I made him some cold lemonade. We talked for a while. I asked his name and age. He told me and again I was shocked. They were the same as in my dream. Then I told him I believed it was by divine chance that he came because I had asked God to give me profound evidence that He had called me to preach. The priest told me God had sent him to come and verify it with me. That is why he got lost; God wanted him to find me.

I still was in denial that afternoon when I arrived home. I called the friends I had called before about the dream. I told them about the actual real happenings of that afternoon. No one doubted me, and they encouraged me to accept the fact that I was divinely called, but I said, "Not yet."

All week I was restless. I couldn't seem to settle down. Every morning at 5 AM I would go for my walk. I loved it at that time because everything smelled so nice and clean and fresh. I would walk to the river first, and I could sit on a huge tree trunk that extended about thirty feet over the water. It was my favorite spot because I could watch the dawn break. It was an awesome sight. I had written many a poem on that tree trunk. I was sorry to see them remove it years later.

Every day I would walk, walk, walk. Sometimes I would have to look back. It seemed as if someone were following me. I became withdrawn. I prayed and fasted so much for answers to my perplexing questions. My husband told me he was afraid I would get sick, but I continued to pray and fast. About three weeks after my encounter with the priest, I went to work and my lady told me she had to be away all afternoon. I had been with her two years and this would be only the second time she would be away while I was there. My, God works in mysterious ways.

About 1:30 I was washing dishes and something came over me. I began to tremble. I heard this preaching, preaching. I knew my soul was being edified. I could feel every atom of my being come alive. I walked from room to room. The preaching continued. I began to sob quite hard. Everywhere I went, the preaching continued. Then the Scripture that the evangelist used when I was baptized in the Holy Spirit was said. I began to speak in tongues as the Scripture, "What have I to render unto the Lord for all His benefits toward me," was expounded on.

The preaching did not stop. I continued walking from room to room. I came to the hall, and there was a mirror. I looked in the mirror and I saw my mouth forming words, tears streaming down my face. It dawned on me that I was the one doing the expounding on the Word. I was so edified that the Scripture, "Oh, taste and see that the Lord is good," and the words that were falling from my lips were like honey. I couldn't stop. I found myself happy and very sad at the same time. Finally, I came down to earth, finished the dishes, and went home.

Down at the river, in my private place, I began to ask the Lord what direction I was to go, now that I had accepted His call. I was led to go to one of my Christian advisers, Rev. Alvin Jackson. This particular man was one of the best teachers I had ever known. I related all that had happened. He was giving a young minister private tutoring and he told me to join the class. He only taught two at a time. I had been to two Bible schools, but I was always ready to learn.

While a few ministers encouraged me and tried to help me, there were those who did not believe in women preachers. My own pastor considered me an oddball and treated me badly. So, it was a consolation as well as an inspiration to have a former teacher available at this critical time.

As the news got out about my call, I began to get a lot of advice from friends, ministers, and even enemies. I went to my pastor and told him what had happened, and I asked him if I could have a date for my trial sermon. He said, "No," that I was just going through a physical change that had affected my thinking. I saw his mind was made up, so I went to two very nice Christian deacons and I explained my situation to them. I told them I would like to have a meeting with the pastor and the board. They arranged it.

The meeting was held. The pastor again said, "No." One of the deacons asked the pastor if he believed in the whole Bible. The pastor said, "Every word is true." The deacon said, "Well, didn't the Lord say He would pour out His blessings on all flesh? Well, Reverend, we know this is the Lord's blessing on our sister. Let us support her for she belongs to us. She came here a twelve-year-old child to this church. We feel she should have her chance." They voted unanimously that I could have my chance.

The invitations went out. My friends came from all over to support me. I was led to go to a friend's home in a consecrated prayer and shut-in. My dear friend Mercy Dawes shut-in with me.

Mercy was a gifted prayer-warrior, with whom I had made many visits to hospitals and nursing homes. I had seen healing and deliverances as the result of her prayers and laying on of hands. I admired her greatly for the work she and her husband did in New York and North Carolina as well as in New Jersey. She was a humble servant of God, who had turned her basement into Holy Ghost "headquarters." It was her inspiration that led me to her home for my important shut-in.

The Lord gave me for my first sermon Acts 1, first chapter, the eleventh verse, "This same Jesus." When I came out of that shut-in and went outside to come home, the world so much brighter. It was as if the Lord was saying, "I love you." My first sermon was a beautiful blessing to me and everyone. I began to receive engagements to preach around the country and also to do my dramatic readings. I enjoyed working for the Lord. My immediate family supported me very well. My pastor usually gave me a hard time. I kept on praying.

Eventually the Lord saw fit to remove him from the charge. After three months our church hired another minister.

My Ministry

I traveled quite a lot. I was called to Norfolk, Virginia where I preached on the radio for Bishop Willis who is now world famous. He's on radio every day, and after all these years, we have remained friends. God really blessed me in a beautiful way. The children were growing up and going to high school. My life had not been a bed of roses. Satan had attacked me every way he could, but I soon learned that "greater is He that is in me than he who is in the world." Sometimes people wounded me with the traps they set for me, but most of them fell in their own traps. They lied, which hurt me the most. The Lord told me long ago that "the battle was not mine, but His if I would just stand still and let Him have the battle alone. He doesn't need me to help him."

All of my immediate family were saved. I had six very dear friends, and we frequently got together for prayer and just to talk. One night I went to bed and I dreamed of three snakes trying to attack me. The next night I dreamed about these same three snakes. I was quite disturbed about it. I called an older, saintly lady. I told her about it. She told me I had some bad enemies. I said, "So, what else is new?" I had plenty of enemies. She said, "Daughter, these three mean you harm." She said, "You fast and pray all day, and tonight when you go to bed ask the Lord to reveal them to you for your protection because He's trying to warn you." She told me any time I had a dream that repeated itself two nights in a row to ask the Lord to reveal its message to me.

I went to bed on the third night after praying and asked the Lord to reveal those snakes to me. Well, that night when those snakes came at me and I saw those faces my heart was broken. They were the faces of three dear friends of mine. I woke my husband because I was crying so hard. All the next day I cried. Why? Why? I had done everything I could to help them. I used my car to take them to revivals. I had given them so much; now I find they wish to harm me. One of them I loved especially. I decided to go to her and find out why she hated me when I loved her so.

I prayed before I went to her. I talked to her with all the love I had for her. She was like a sister to me. "Why do you hate me and wish me harm?" I asked her. She was shocked when I told her. She burst out crying, and told me she hated me so bad. She and her friends had been praying for my death. Can you imagine the shock that was to me? She said they were jealous because the Lord had blessed me so and hadn't done anything for them. I made up my mind I was not going to the other two. This girlfriend poured it all out. She broke down and asked me to please forgive her. I told her I had forgiven her by coming to her. We both cried in each other's arms. I went home feeling much better. I was glad I had gone to her.

I tried loving those other two ladies more and more. One of them repented, but the other one after seventeen years still has the same feelings toward me and is still smiling in my face.

The prayer band that we had formed had to have meetings in a high school now because it was so big. It developed into a church. There were two churches found in our living room. My pastor and I were on a better footing than we were before. One Sunday morning during service, he called me out of the choir. He presented me with a legal license for preaching he dated back from 1968. My life was changing for the better. I was appointed Director of Welfare in our town, a job I enjoyed because I loved serving people.

Not too long after that I had a dream that changed hundreds of lives. The Lord has used me in some mighty big ways. I dreamed I saw this gigantic man standing with both legs spread from one end of my town to the other. He was pulling people out of sewer gutters and the slimy muck and mire. This dream persisted on the next day. On the third night, I asked the Lord to reveal the man's face because it seemed as if it were a message. Sure enough, on that third night, I had the same dream, except there was a light going up his legs. When his face was revealed, I was pleasantly surprised: It was Pastor Benjamin Smith of Deliverance Evangelistic Church in Philadelphia.

For a few days I pondered on what the dream meant. I had a prayer band going on in my home every Friday, and the Lord really blessed us. I asked the Lord what did He want me to do about it. The answer came. I wrote a ten-page letter to Dr. Benjamin Smith in Philadelphia. I told him my dream and other things that had happened, how we were praying for our city, and how one of the saints of the prayer band had a vision. The Lord told her He was going to deliver this city. I received a telephone call from Benjamin Smith, and we talked and made plans for him to come to my home.

One afternoon, my best friend, Louise Jackson, visited me. I told her about the dream and while we were talking, another friend came by. I told her about the dream. Louise said she had been thinking about the minister a lot lately. The second friend said she had seen a member of his church. We had a prayer meeting as we usually did when we got together. On the day after Labor Day in 1972, Benjamin Smith and his associates came to my home. I called my two friends and they came, and after we talked over my dream, Rev. Smith said truly the Lord had guided me through the whole thing.

We planned a two-day revival meeting for the coming month. We had to use a movie house because we could not find a church big enough for the busloads. We had ninety-eight youth each day. We really heard from the Lord. Rev. Smith let me announce that my prayer meetings were held at my home on Fridays. After that, my home was filled with people every Friday, including a young man who came every week. We traveled with a witnessing party all over Burlington County, and our mission was quite successful.

I was still quite busy with speaking engagements. Through these meetings, Rev. Smith introduced me to a beautiful couple, Ellen amd Ted Grant, who became dear friends of my husband and me. Today Ellen is still one of my dearest friends, who has stayed by me through deaths in my family, through tears of happiness, failures, and hurts.

When the Lord blesses, the devil messes. One evening after dinner, my husband called my name and it sounded strange. On the next day, it happened again. I remarked about it. He said everything was fine. Days went by. I saw a shadow on his neck that no one could see, not even the doctor. Everyone said I had an overactive imagination, but I heard the strange voice and that dark spot was still there in my sight. The doctor said he just gained too much weight. I could not rest. I was disturbed in my spirit. I called a specialist and insisted on him seeing my husband right away. He asked who recommended him.

I told him, "The Holy Spirit told me."

He asked, "What doctor?"

I said, "Our doctor didn't believe me when I told him about my husband. He tried to put a tube down John's throat, but he could not because something in the throat would not let the tube through."

An appointment was made for John to be seen in the hospital the next day. They put him to sleep and ran several tests. After two days had passed, the specialist asked me to come to his office alone. I knew already that something was wrong. I was prayed up when I went to see the doctor. It's a good thing because they told me what I expected. He had advanced cancer of the throat, and it looked as if it had spread elsewhere.

I didn't tell him for two days. John and I were very close and we could tell when something was wrong. I took him down to the river for a walk. We sat in the gazebo, and I told him all about it. I told him he needed an operation right away. He said, "All right, if it means that we can be together longer, I want it."

We went to the specialist to talk. I asked the doctor which hospital would he send his wife to if she were in John's shoes. He told me, and we said, "Make the arrangements." Two days later he went to the hospital in Philadelphia. He was in there three weeks taking radiation treatments before he was operated on. We had set up a prayer vigil all over the USA and India. John went through a seventeen-hour, radical, major operation. He went through it with no problems, such as fever or infection. When they called me in for a conference, they told me it had spread so bad they couldn't get it all. They had to take his voice box out. They said with luck he could live six months. I told them "not so," he had been completely healed, and do not give him that doomsday information. He had been in the hospital one month.

I had to let my prayer band be moved to another home, because I had to stay at the hospital every moment I could. I lived twenty-five miles away. My sister Lucy took care of our children, which was a blessing. The members of the Deliverance Evangelistic Church in Philadelphia went to see John all the time he was in the hospital. They prayed, anointed, and laid hands on him. He really responded well. After we came home, at least ten people would come by to pray for John every day. I stayed with him and took care of him. He could not talk, so he went to a class that taught him esophageal speech.

I continued preaching. I was doing so much. After John was home for one month, I had a pain in my chest. I went to the doctor. He gave me medicine. It didn't do me any good. John went outside to sit on the porch. I was lying on the floor and suddenly felt strange and weak. I couldn't get up to call John. I called the doctor, who sent the ambulance right away, which frightened John when it stopped at our home. They got me to the hospital pronto.

I was one sick lady. All of the stress, deaths, work, and worry had taken its toll. Rheumatic fever undiagnosed as a child had played its part in making me susceptible. They thought I was going to die. Six of my prayer partners, including a doctor friend, encamped around my bed in the Intensive Care Unit until three o'clock in the morning. They anointed and prayed for me, and after seventeen days the good Lord sent me back to do more work for Him. I had had a major heart attack.

John and I recuperated together. I had to take it easy for quite a while. It was hard because I had always been very active. Everyone was so good to us. They would come by and anoint us with holy water and oil every day. I missed our prayer band very much. When we went to the hospital for John's monthly checkup, the doctor called another doctor to confer. They said the area of John's throat looked very clean. After six months, the doctors said they couldn't believe it: they could not find any trace of cancer on John. We knew what had happened, and we praised the Lord for it. From the very moment of John's problem he never had an ache or pain nor a fever. He was really a miracle.

Against the doctor's advice, I began accepting preaching engagements and the Lord blessed me.

John lived ten years after his cancer operation. He had a clean bill of health. Life went on, and our children were growing up. Our son Donald was in sports and loved playing baseball. John always traveled to see all of his games.

One afternoon after dinner, John and I went to the river to see our son play ball. John sat in the bleachers; I sat in the car at the end of the field reading. Donald was in center field. I looked up to see Donald running, and everyone started to run to the bleachers. I knew that it was John by the time I got there. He was in a bad way. On the way to the hospital, John died in my arms, saying my name. Denial set in. Numbness and unbelief took over, but it was true. John had died of a cerebral hemorrhage. My beloved was gone. John died before seeing his favorite baseball player's children: Donald was later to give me additional grandchildren, Gina and Christina.

Our daughter Kimberly was in college and was engaged to be married. John had been looking forward to giving our youngest child in marriage. He would have looked so handsome in his formal attire. I thanked God for this important diversion from my grief. The plans took up all of my spare time. I didn't have time to feel sorry for myself because I was too busy.

The day of the wedding was beautiful. The sun shone brightly and the weather was mild. Everyone came. It was a happy and sad occasion because it was less than three months since John passed away, and it was almost impossible to retain my composure watching Kimberly come down the aisle on her uncle Earl Morris' arm; he was identical in looks to her father. Both of them were crying very hard. All of the girls and the whole wedding party were beautiful. The bride was marrying Eduardo Hernandez, a very handsome Spanish fellow, and the wedding was a colorful rainbow wedding.

After their honeymoon, the newlyweds came back to their own apartment. I really hit a low as the loss of John sank in. I was so lonely in that empty, ten-room home that we had bought when Butch needed a fenced yard to play in.

New Missions—New Life

Everybody had left home. I was completely alone. I poured myself into every Christian activity I could. I became a member of the South Jersey Evangelistic Conference, and I really was blessed. My phone was still on twenty-four hour prayer time. When I wasn't traveling to Norfolk, Virginia, I was traveling to New York. The Lord sent me plenty of work to do for Him. I was asked to write, produce, and direct several dramas that were quite successful.

I began to notice a severe tightening in my chest. It concerned me because I have always had a chronic cough and shortness of breath. One night I woke up and it seemed as if an elephant was standing on my chest. I called the paramedics, then crawled downstairs and called my children. When I woke up, I was in the Intensive Care Unit. I realized I had overdone it again. My family was frightened, but I told them I was not afraid, to call all the prayer-warriors and let them know I am here and everything will be alright. All of the saints responded to my call and came to me. I know beyond a shadow of a doubt that the prayers of the righteous availeth much. I remained under intensive cardiac care.

One afternoon while I was in a half-sleep in the hospital, I looked out of the window of my room. There were two hills. A barrel was at the top of each hill. After a while, the one on the left side started to roll downhill. When it was rolling, there was the loudest clanging noise I have ever heard. When it reached bottom, it cracked open and all these people fell out of that barrel. I knew all of them. They were all saved people. There were ministers, evangelists, and a lot of fancy-dressed saints whom I had always looked up to. I wondered what it all meant. Well, I looked to the hill on the right and that barrel was rolling downhill without any noise at all. It got to the bottom and opened. The people got out and I recognized a lot of little saints, plain-dressed and very low-keyed, whom I had overlooked. These people didn't make any noise in church. I wondered what it meant.

The next day I told one of my visitors about the dream or vision, and I asked her what could she make of it. She said the Lord was letting me know the people I looked up to were as sounding brass and tinkling symbols. The second barrel were the true saints. What a lesson I learned about saints. I continued to mend and soon returned home. Many a saint called me and asked me which barrel he or she was in. It was really funny, but of course I didn't tell them. Some of them would sure be surprised!

I tried keeping myself busy in my Christian work. I met so many beautiful saints over the years and have made many lifetime friendships. It seemed as if Satan really wanted to kill me. Every time I was doing good work for the Lord, I would get knocked off my feet. At the time everyone was being warned to take the swine flu shot. My doctor told me that, since I had this respiratory problem and had had two heart attacks, I should have the shot. I was a little concerned because every time I took a shot for a particular illness I got the disease. Three saints called and told me they were led to call and tell me not to take the shot, but I became concerned because of my health. I decided to take the shot.

Two weeks later, on a Sunday morning while sitting in the choir, I became quite disoriented. I remember feeling sad and began to cry for no reason at all. I got up and walked out of church in my choir robe, leaving my coat and purse in church. I went home and laid on the couch in my robe. All day long I heard people talking to me, but I couldn't respond. I fell asleep. My girlfriend Lou came in and called my daughters. It was as if I were looking at someone else in that condition.

That night when evening service was over at church, everyone came by to see me. I was still in my robe. All of a sudden they told me I screamed, "Jesus, have mercy on me!" That was all I remember for two days. I was taken to the hospital that Sunday night. The doctors fought for my life. The saints prayed and prayed. I was in and out of consciousness for days. Finally, the crisis passed, and for five days I kept asking what was wrong. They wouldn't tell me until the day I was discharged. They told me I had come very close to being a statistic. I had contracted swine flu, and during that whole winter only four of the people who had contracted it in the state had survived and I was one of them. Praise God.

It took me quite a long time to get myself together, but the Lord was good to me. I was soon back on the battlefield for my Lord.

The days and nights were still very lonely. I was traveling to Norfolk and Portsmouth, Virginia, working for the Lord. One day while I was resting at home, three ministers from Pennsylvania, New Jersey, and Delaware came to my home. They told me about a club of ten ministers and evangelists they were forming and wanted me to join them. I was very flattered and told them I would let them know. After fasting and praying on it, I decided against it.

A few weeks later, they invited me to be in a service. It was one of the most interesting services I have ever participated in. It was called a Spiritual Round Robin. They told me to fast and study the Scriptures because I would not know what subject or Scripture I would have to expound on. Six evangelists are chosen and the mediators throw out Scripture at random to us in front of a congregation. You have three minutes to expound. This goes on for about an hour and a half. It keeps you on your toes. It is very entertaining also. I thoroughly enjoyed it.

While the work of the Lord was fulfilling, I still had much time on my hands. My daughter Kim and family had moved away, and I was alone.

Loneliness

I hadn't seen my daughter Peggy's children and my great-grandchildren in quite a while. My two grandchildren Lenni and Princess had been sent overseas for two years with their respective spouses, who were in the Air Force. Now they were living in California. They begged me to visit them for an indefinite stay. So, in February of 1991, I purchased my ticket, keeping my plan a secret.

One Sunday while on my way to church, I had a flat tire and was waiting for the mechanic to come and fix it. A beautiful gray Lincoln car pulled up, and this gray-headed gentleman, six foot two, stepped out. He was dressed in a white suit and wore a light blue shirt. He was really handsome. I was dressed almost identical to him. He came and offered to fix my tire. I told him I was expecting the mechanic. We began to talk, and I told him he looked familiar. He said

I did also, and when I told him my name, he asked me my maiden name, and when I told him Margaret Hicks, he told me his name, James Henderson, and we both laughed and hugged each other. He was the fellow who stole his mother's handkerchiefs and gave them to me and who wrote me little love notes when we were in the third and fourth grades, back in Riverside, New Jersey.

We had a most delightful time. He went with me to church, and after church we brought my car home. We rode around and went to see our old school—and had a good laugh. We had dinner at an outdoor restaurant, and everything was delightful. He told me whom he had married and I told him whom I had married. We both knew each other's spouses, and we found out that both of our spouses had died eight years earlier, and we both were alone. It was a coincidence that we met in New Jersey because he lived in Virginia.

James asked if he could he call me on the phone. He called the next day, and from then on he called me at least four times a week. We had long telephone conversations, and he sent me flowers every week. My favorite flowers were yellow roses, the same kind John used to give me.

James was retired and could come to see me quite often. He was a beautiful dresser, which I appreciated because I, too, liked to dress well. We could really turn heads when we went out. I liked going to good restaurants, and he took me to the best. We had a most delightful time when we were together. I showed him a perfume bottle he gave me when I was in the fourth grade. I showed him a ribbon he had given me. He stole all of these things from his mother. The perfume was Evening in Paris. I was thrilled to receive perfume at that age. He was impressed that I kept everything.

I was working part-time doing social work. I had my own office, and many a time I would look up and see this handsome man standing in the doorway with flowers or candy. My co-workers were really jealous.

The holidays and my birthday were coming up, and I was planning a large Thanksgiving with my children and James. They all liked him and he liked them. We were celebrities when we went out. We were senior citizens, and we walked around holding hands like teenagers. We were teased a lot. After dinner, James asked all of the children and grands to come around. He took a beautiful box out of his pocket, and he asked the children would they become his step-children and grandchildren. Everybody said, "YES!" He still hadn't asked me! They all turned to me after hugging him, saying, "We accept you." Of course, what else could I do but accept.

News traveled fast, and the phone rang and rang. We planned a wedding for the following spring. I continued my plan to visit California. I informed my children and James that I was going to California to visit Pegeen's children, Lenni and Princess. Both were married and Lenni and John Brown, Princess' husband, were stationed at the same Air Force base. Lenni and his wife Diahne had two children, Lenny, Jr., and Donisha. Princess Evans had three children, Angela, April, and John, Jr. I hated to leave James. He said this would give him time to do a lot of things that needed doing.

Westward Ho!

The family saw me off on my journey to California. I traveled by train, taking three days to get there. Cities and towns, bridges and dams—man's great works were inspiring. But the greatest experience was seeing God's handwork: the pine trees that seemed to be fifty feet tall, aspen trees with their white branches and trunks as white as snow—to see them for miles and miles in the mountains looking like snow—the creeks and rivers winding in and out of the mountains and valleys, the white snowy clouds looking like great big puffs of cotton floating around mountaintops, the variety of animals coming to drink at the water's edge—miles and miles of cactus, some as high as six feet with their beautiful blooms—seeing trout jumping up in the streams and the swift white-capped currents used for water rafting—the sun shining and the temperature at 98°, snowcapped mountains and gorgeous homes sticking out from the cliffs—everything was awesome. I had to cry.

I saw sights I had never seen before. I saw the route of the Pony Express. I could imagine seeing riders chased by Indians. There were so many wonderful things to see. The six-mile tunnel, the Donner Pass. It was wonderful.

The New Generations

It was a marvelous visit with Pegeen's children, Lenni and Princess and my great-grandchildren. They had planned a lovely vacation for me. Although they had to work, they arranged it so one of the four adults was with me all the time. Princess' husband, John, took off two days and spent them with me. We went to see Alcatraz. It was very interesting. I was able to sit on the cot that Baby Face Nelson slept on, and I went into the cell of many a criminal. It was a queer feeling to touch the cell of the Bird Man of Alcatraz. I saw the cells occupied by Al Capone and Machine Gun Kelly. Even the ferry ride to the Island was interesting, and it prompted him to take me on a cruise. We cruised San Francisco Bay, passing under its great bridge that connects San Francisco to Oakland. It was a peaceful ride.

I spent much time with my five great-grands. They showed me their school and the neighborhood, and they were very proud to show off their great-grandma who could outwalk them and jump rope and ride a bicycle. The children of the neighborhood told their parents to come and meet me. It was a busy time, but there were moments for reflectful rest. My reputation for barbecues and planning large family outings was not forgotten. They insisted that I prepare a picnic for their families and friends on the base.

On Sunday we all went to church on the base. They were beautiful services, and I really enjoyed them. Sunday afternoon we were invited to spend with friends. They were all amazed that I could swim so well at my age. Sundays seemed to be specially blessed.

And so the days and weeks were filled with laughter and love— grandchildren and great grands, new generations in new environments, strikingly different from my life back East. I had saved my money for this trip and had built my plans. But my children went far beyond my wishes and expectations in welcoming me into their homes. It was especially pleasing to meet their many friends and experience the rich harmony of their lives. One occasion was particularly touching: Two beautiful Caucasian girls came to visit me. They had heard about a prayer breakfast I had been to and that I had given the Invocation and testified. They came for prayer and an unbiased counseling on a problem one of them was having. They both were saved, and it was a most rewarding meeting.

My grandchildren generously took me to Hollywood and a studio tour, to Los Angeles restaurants and a Chinese barbecue. Donisha and Lenny, Jr. took me to shops and flea markets. They all found many other things that they knew I would enjoy doing. The four adults and seven children were determined to make my vacation memorable—and they did.

Their farewell dinner was very special—warm and intimate. The great-grandchildren begged me to tell them stories.

"Grandma, tell us some of the stories from your poor days when you were young in the South." I laughed and said, "I wasn't poor. We had plenty of food and clothing and a lot of joy and happiness and lots of love."

"Well," I said, "I'm going to tell you about the time I was about six years old:

My cousin Ervin and cousin Snooks and myself and my sister knee-baby Nell, were playing down in the field by the meadow and our dog Dash was running about. We all were so happy and carefree and warm and barefoot playing in the grass. We came to a patch of weeds growing, and Ervin said, "Here is a lot of rabbit tobacco." Someone asked did rabbits chew it, and Ervin asked how did they smoke it, and Snooks said, "They take the leaves that is dried and put in paper and roll it up and light it."

We went back to the house and we got some funny papers. Today we call them comics. I can remember it so well, because it was a full page of Orphan Annie. We took some matches, and Mama made me take my baby sister Vi out with us. Of course, she didn't know what we were about to do. We went back to the field and gathered some dry rabbit tobacco leaves. We tore strips of paper, put the leaves on them, rolled them up, and spit on the ends to make them stick. We made of a lot of them and Ervin, Snooks, and I lit them and gave them to everyone. Snooks and Ervin taught us how to smoke, and after much coughing and gagging, we got the hang of it. Then you have never heard so much giggling and laughing in all your life! Baby Vi and knee-baby Nell could hardly stand up. They fell on the ground screaming and laughing. Ervin began to dance crazily and Snooks stood on her head laughing the whole time. I was floating on air and, all of a sudden, Orphan Annie and Sandy became good friends. We began to dance together, and I laughed and laughed. I couldn't stop. I don't know how long we stayed out there or when we finished our cigarettes. We were floating in another world.

We stayed so long in the field Mama called us in to eat. I didn't meet my Papa coming home from work as I usually did. We all floated to the house. Mama told us to wash up for supper. All the time we were giggling. We sat down to eat. We were still giggling. Papa said, "We will pray and ask God's blessing on our food." Well, we really cracked up then. You didn't dare lift your eyes or hardly breathe when Papa's praying, and here we are screaming with laughter! Everyone looked from one to another of us in wonder. Papa said, "Ahem!" two or three times. We still couldn't stop laughing. Papa said, "Youngins, what's ailing you?" We laughed harder.

Then Ervin said, "There's Dash and he is grinning, and there is another dog with him on the porch!"

Odell said, "There's no other dog there but Dash."

Snooks said, "It's Sandy!!"

We all began to squeal, "Sandy, Sandy!"

Then I said, "Look! There's Orphan Annie and Daddy Warbucks!"

The table was in shock as the gang of us ran to the door to play with Dash, Sandy, and Orphan Annie. We danced around the room as if we were playing with someone. Finally, we were getting tired and sleepy.

Mama said, "Papa, they are acting crazy. I'd better give them some castor oil." We went into peals of laughter, and fell on the floor laughing.

I said, "I'll take it first!" They knew something was wrong because we all hated castor oil, and we would hide when we had to take it. They gave us all castor oil and put us to bed, cousins and all. We would wake up during the night, laughing and giggling. Well, you can imagine what went on all night on the chamber pot. Papa had to take it to the outhouse twice and wash it out.

When we all got up the next day, we could not get enough to eat. Everyone was looking at us. I said, "Mama, I've had the queerest dream," and everyone said the same thing. Ervin said, "I dreamed we were down in the field smoking cigarettes." Mama and my brother Charles looked at each other. Charles went out and came back in with part of the comics and some burnt matches. Mama, Odell, and Charles laughed until they cried. We thought they had lost their minds. When Papa came home and Mama told Papa what they had found, he too laughed, and they sat us down and told us never to touch rabbit tobacco again, that it was poison, and God would punish us. That's all he had to tell me because I was so scared of God. His name could make me tremble. This is before I learned about the loving, compassionate God. Well, that day we ate and ate and ate. We felt queer all day long. I never saw Orphan Annie again in my entire life. After that experience, I never wanted to see her or Sandy again!

A few weeks later when the whole field of rabbit tobacco dried out, I and our gang and the whole town had a similar experience. Early one evening, Papa and Charles and some men burned the whole field. We learned later in life that the rabbit tobacco was probably a field of wild marijuana! I believe we were the youngest to ever smoke marijuana.

My great-grandchildren loved the story. Everyone was laughing so hard they were crying. "Grandma, tell us the one about the lightning bugs, please Grandma, please!"

Everyone was begging me to tell them another of my childhood adventures. So I said to Princess, who was expecting her third child, "I'll tell them one more story. This is about how my Mama nearly had ten children instead on nine." It went like this:

In the South when I was about six years old, my cousins Ervin, Delmus, Alisee, and my sister knee-baby Nell, and I were playing in the yard. Old Lady Whitney, who was a midwife, was coming down the dusty road with her black bag and a big stick she used as a cane. She always dressed in black. We were in awe of her because we were told she was carrying a baby in that black bag! She was always walking hard and fast. We children started in back of her; she turned around and we ran back to my house.

I guess we were playing for about two hours,

when Old Lady Bumbry came by. We heard her tell Mama that Miss Lila would not have the baby, and Old Lady Whitney was trying to make her have it. We kids sneaked down and put our faces in the fence. We heard all this screaming going on, and Miss Lila was scream-ing, "No! No! No!" That kept on for a while.

I said to them, "What is going on? It's awful."

Alisee said, "Miss Lila don't want it. She's beating Miss Lila with the stick trying to make her take the baby."

That noise kept on so long. I told the kids I was sure my Mama would take the baby, and Old Lady Whitney would not have to hit her with that stick! I said, "Let's go tell Miss Whitney Mama will take the baby! We went to the door and Ervin knocked gingerly. A woman came to the door, and I said in my little scared voice, "Tell Miss Whitney not to beat Miss Lila anymore. Mama will take the baby."

Well, that lady let out a whoop and started to laugh real hard. Then she shushed us up, and told us we had better get home or we would get a whipping. It got back to Mama, and she and some of the ladies were laughing about it. But, she never set me straight about it.

The next day my brother was teasing me about trying to get us another baby. All the older ones laughed. When I had my first child, I knew by then it wasn't going to be delivered in a little black bag, and no one was going to beat me with a stick.

Everyone was almost rolling in the floor by the time I was fin-ished telling this escapade!

My great-grands and I sat on the floor after the stories and talked. They asked me to move to California, but I knew I couldn't do that. I went to bed for the last night in California. I was excited about going home because there is still no place like home, but I was also very sad to leave California and the children.

The next day I awoke to one of the most beautiful mornings I have ever seen. The sun was shining in my window. I awoke early and went outside and sat on the steps. It was very quiet. The homes on the Air Force base were lovely; there were palm trees and flowers everywhere. After a while, I felt little arms slip about my neck. It was my two precious little great-granddaughters, April and Angela. They both started talking at the same time. One would start a sentence, and the other would chime in to finish it or add to it. Their patter went like this:

"No, Greatmother, you weren't poor when you were little—you had your Mommy and Daddy and cousins and uncles and aunts—who all loved you—and played with you—and you had your church and picnics—and all that singing—you didn't have toys—but you had different things—you had meadows and creeks—and animals—they were better than toys—you weren't poor."

I realized that my greatgrands had been talking to their parents. I realized, too, how much I was loved today. And, although there were tears in my eyes, I knew—oh, I knew, I wasn't poor, ever.

We sat huddled on that step. They said, "Grandma, don't leave, please stay with us." I hugged them and promised to see them real soon. [Six months after I left California they were transferred to Okinawa.]

When it was time to go to the train, we all piled into one car, but before we left I blessed and prayed for the whole household as I usually do when leaving homes. We had to drive forty-five miles to get to the train. We all were crying. We had to wait about a half hour before my train came. How very quiet and sad it was, and we fidgeted and moved around nervously. At the departure gates, we all hugged and kissed each other and held each other real tight. We tried not to cry. I took my seat and sat looking out and waving from the window. Finally, "All aboard!", and we began to move.

The trip back from the West Coast was more reflective. The beautiful scenery was there and the weather was bright, but my thoughts moved back to the many incidents in my life and how God had always been present. And many of his saints on earth were there to help me make decisions and manage through difficult times.

After my wonderful family—my Mama and Papa, my brother and sisters, the spiritual friends that I made throughout the years come to mind. But both helped me realize that I always needed to be with and helping people if I could. So there were others for whom I worked who are today dearly remembered. The Fentons who saw John and me through the trying days of Butch's illness. Dear to me are the David Spicca family, whose huge farm and huge heart helped my family materially. And there are the Halls—Rupert and Anne and their darling children who are so special to me today.

What I seemed to need so often in my life was an extended family. Life was lonesome in 1989; my husband was dead, my children were married and in their own homes, and I was alone in a ten-room house. I missed the little ones, and I know my true vocation was so much more to be with people.

As a young girl, I looked after Nell and Vi and, after moving to New Jersey, I looked forward to minding my big sister Nina's children. Even before I had my own children, I had the opportunity to nurture a young relative of my husband's, Pat Mills. A darling girl, Pat visited us from Brooklyn and later came to live with us. She became my first "granddaughter." I have always wanted or needed children around me.

Providentially, Rupert Hall, a successful attorney, and his wife Anne, a dedicated special needs teacher, needed a babysitter. I answered their advertisement.

As I sat in the driveway of the Hall home, I felt as if I had already known their place. I cannot explain the joy I experienced when this beautiful black couple answered my knock. She was holding the most adorable seven-month-old baby girl and had two cute little boys at her side, two and a half years old and five years old. Their smiles lit up the room, and I was dying to hold the baby. While we were talking, the baby lifted up her hands, and I took her in my hungry arms. She snuggled quickly on my neck. The Lord worked in mysterious ways. He put that family and me together, my new extended family. I acquired another daughter and another son and three babies. They told me they had their church praying along with them that God would send them a Christian woman to take care of their babies. Today that Christian family and my immediate family are dear friends. Their family in the South has become my family. The children are all in school now; two have outgrown their need for me, but they still love me and I love them. They will always be part of my family.

Rudy and Anne and their children, Brigette, Roland, and Arland Halley certainly filled the void in my life. I see these wonderful people frequently, but it is no surprise to me that they occupied my thoughts on much of my long trip back home. I had left the love of my blood relations in California, knowing that I would never be lonely in the East with the blessed Hall family to love and be loved by.

My journey was over, and my thoughts were once again interrupted by words that had played such a big part in my life sixty-four years ago. "Next stop is Thirtieth Street Station, Philadelphia! Next stop is Thirtieth Street Station!" The conductor called out, "We are coming into Thirtieth Street Station!"

I collected my luggage and walked down the aisle, wondering who would meet me this time. My mind kept going back to that time sixty-four years ago, as I stepped down. It wasn't Mama and Papa's faces that I saw this time. It was my beautiful younger daughter Kim, her husband Eduardo, and children Yolanda, Felō, and Marissa waiting with outstretched arms. We all embraced and started walking toward the car, when my daughter said, "Mom, who is that looking at you? Turn around and see." I turned around and looked into the eyes of this great, big, handsome man who had asked me to marry him. Without hesitation, I walked into the loving arms of James, whom I knew was my future.

"To My God Be The Glory"

dear friends, Mr. and Mrs. Fenton. I felt an urge to return to New Jersey even though I had planned to stay another week. I was numb going back to our room. My head was getting stuffy. The rest of the day passed in a haze.

I called Mr. Swales and told him my plans. We would leave the next day if we could get a train out. He told me not to worry, he would take care of it. I said goodbye to all my neighbors. Everyone came to see me off, and we took a lot of pictures. Mr. Swales came with Rev. Fisher to take us to the station. I thanked everyone and told them God was going to bless them for their kindness and support.

Suicide Attempt

By the time we were settled on the train, I was feeling quite ill. I fed my son when we arrived home and made calls to my sisters. Then I locked all the doors and fell unconscious to the floor.

I came to in the emergency ward.

When I hadn't answered the front door, my sisters had looked through the window. They broke in and called my husband. They took me to the hospital, burning up with fever, almost incoherent. The weather in Canada and the disappointment in the outcome of the visit was more than I could take, and it took its toll on my weakened body. I nearly had bronchitis and was on the verge of another breakdown.

The days that followed were hazy and indistinct. God knew I needed a good physical and mental rest. The first Saturday after I left the hospital, the whole clan came to our home to hear about our trip to Canada. My sisters brought covered dishes, and we had a good time. We hadn't gotten together in a long time. Our families had gotten so big.

Butch was still having very bad seizures. They were getting worse every day. He had contracted a fever, and he had seizures for two days. I had not slept in nearly thirty hours. I sent John off to work and Pegeen off to school. I told my husband I slept during the day, but I didn't. I was in a fog. I cooked and cleaned. I bathed and changed Butch until I thought I would drop. "If only someone would come and sit by his bed," I thought, "so I could get some rest." But everyone was frightened of my son's seizures. I could understand it, because they were horrible to see. I had to keep awake to save him from choking to death on his tongue. Afterward, his body was coma-locked, immobile. After dealing with over fifty seizures without sleep, I lost